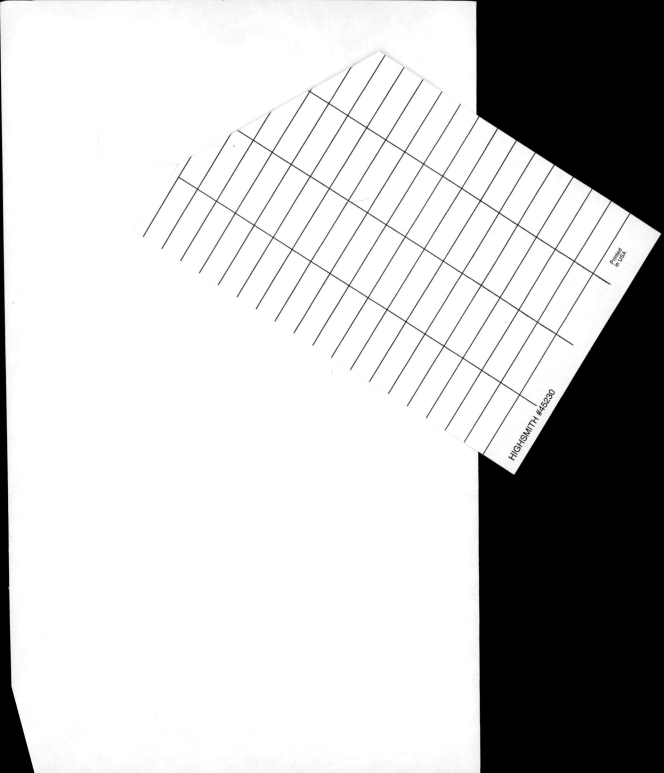

HIGHSMITH #45230

Printed in USA

The Busy Christian's Guide to the Deeper Life

*Twelve Weeks to
Enjoying God More*

WILLIAM D. WATKINS

VINE
BOOKS

Servant Publications
Ann Arbor, Michigan

Vine Books is an imprint of Servant Publications especially designed to serve evangelical Christians.

Published by Servant Publications
P.O. Box 8617
Ann Arbor, Michigan 48107

Cover design: Brian Fowler, DesignTeam, Grand Rapids, MI

Printed in the United States of America
ISBN 0-89283-945-7

Dedication

To my wife, Pamela, whose example awakened in me a thirst to drink more deeply from the well of Christian spirituality.

To Howard Hendricks, whose insightful teaching on Bible study methods opened new vistas of scriptural understanding I am still exploring with inestimable delight.

"We live in a time of spiritual awakening, when many desire a deeper walk with God. *The Busy Christian's Guide to the Deeper Life* combines the clarity of the written word with the heart of a spiritual mentor. Written in an engaging and personal style and from a broadly evangelical perspective, the reader is taken on an evenly-paced journey into the spiritual disciplines. Fortunately, Watkins does not try to introduce something new, rather he introduces the Christian to those practices and attitudes that for centuries have proven to be how God introduces us to something new—a deeper relationship with Him."

–Michael P. Green
Associate Professor of Practical Theology
Trinity Evangelical Divinity School

"The Busy Christian's Guide to the Deeper Life uses a very accessible, hands-on approach to a topic that is often somewhat threatening and guilt-inducing to the average person. Bill Watkins does an admirable job of creating a user-friendly book for busy people in our time and culture, combining solid theology, a rich use of illustrations, and practical exercises. This guide is a good tool to develop the disciplines which are the keys to freedom and intimacy with God."

–Dr. Kenneth D. Boa, Ph.D., D. Phil
President of Reflections Ministries, Inc., Atlanta, Georgia,
author *Unraveling the Big Questions about God,*
I'm Glad You Asked, Talk Thru the Bible, and
Cults, World Religions, and the Occult.

Contents

Acknowledgments

Any work is a team effort. This one is no exception. In that regard I would like to express my gratitude to several people for their assistance.

Many thanks to Pamela Watkins, David Petschulat, and John Dwyer for their review of early and incomplete drafts of this book. I incorporated many of their suggestions, and the book improved as a result.

My appreciation is also extended to Servant Publications for their belief in this project. I especially thank Don Cooper for his enthusiasm and time; Bert Ghezzi for his encouragement and grace; Beth Feia for her diligence and kindness; Heidi Hess for her understanding and patience; and Gwen Ellis for her gentle boldness and support. They demonstrate what Christian professionalism is really about.

Finally, I want to express my abiding gratefulness to my wife, Pamela, and my children—Krista, Jared, Shannon, Hillary, and Katie. Over the years they have all sacrificed to give me the time and solitude I need to study and write. Without their support, none of my writing would ever see the light of day. Whatever value my work has, much of the credit for it goes to them.

The Race:
Discipline and the Deeper Life

Run in such a way as to get the prize.
PAUL THE APOSTLE

PASTOR CHUCK SWINDOLL stood before his congregation and spoke with passion: "As much as I love this church, and I love it dearly, it is a church still in spiritual adolescence. After almost twenty years of serving here as your pastor, it boggles my mind that we have not moved farther down the road together than this."

How could he say such a thing?

During the mid 1980s, my family and I lived in Southern California and did what many other Christians did on a Sunday morning—attended the packed services of the First Evangelical Free Church of Fullerton, where Charles Swindoll was the pastor. At the time, I was serving as the director of educational resources for his radio ministry, Insight for Living.

Chuck's church and parachurch ministry were thriving. On Sundays, the church held four services, three in the morning and one in the evening. At each service as many as 2,500 people would be seated within the sanctuary while several hundred sat in an overflow chapel rigged with televisions and audio so worshipers could at least see and hear the worship service. Even with these accommodations, hundreds of people were turned away each service due to lack of space. Sunday school classes and nursery facilities were also used to capacity.

Insight for Living (IFL) was growing at an incredible rate as well. At that time, IFL's programming was on more than 250 radio stations nationwide, and in many localities each program aired twice a day, five days per week. IFL's active mailing list was about 300,000 strong, and its study guides were selling 1.2 million copies per year.

Now here was this much-loved pastor telling his congregation they were immature in the Lord. Something was missing, something significant. But what? We were a praying church, a Bible-focused church, a worshiping church, a fellowshiping church, a counseling church; and we had the most envied pastor in America preaching to us week after week. What was missing?

What we lacked was *discipline in the Christian life*.

The prayer, Bible study, worship, and fellowship that occurred in the church on Sundays rarely found expression during the rest of the week. It wasn't that the congregation wasn't interested in praying more, or studying our Bibles more, or any of the rest of it. It was that our lives were so frantic, so stressed from Monday through Saturday that we had little time and even less energy to put into our spiritual development. Consequently, we had grown to spiritual adolescence but could grow no further. Maturity lay just beyond our grasp. And it would remain that way until our commitment to Christ would get going with a disciplined lifestyle.

A Runner Named Paul

The apostle Paul understood this truth about the spiritual life. He believed that all Christians were runners in a race. He asked believers, "Do you not know that in a race all the runners run but only one gets the prize? Run in such a way as to get the prize" (1 Cor 9:23-24). In other words, run to win! Be a competitor. Don't be lazy. Don't hold back. Paul's understanding of the Christian life does not promote a passive "let go and let God" approach. Rather, his view represents more of an active "get going with God" strategy. Paul sees Christians as runners in a race, not as bench-warming spectators. As runners, we are not to be Sunday-only athletes, the weekend warriors of sports. Christians are to train every day, week in and week out. And our training must be disciplined and rigorous.

Don't think that God does it all and you do nothing. Give the race all you have. Compete hard. Go after not fourth, third, or even second place, but first place.

What does it take to win? In Paul's words, it takes "strict training" (v. 25) and running with purpose. "I do not run like a man running aimlessly," he said. "I beat my body and make it my slave so that after I have preached to others, I myself will not be disqualified for the prize" (vv. 26-27). Paul realized that continued growth in godliness demanded he work to discipline his life.

What was the prize Paul strove to win? It is "a crown that will last forever" (v. 25). In another letter he describes this crown as "the crown of righteousness, which the Lord, the righteous Judge, will award to me on that day—and not only to me, but also to all who have longed for his appearing" (2 Tim 4:8).[1] Not all Christians will receive this crown. It will go to those who have stepped out of the stands and come onto the playing field to train and compete according to God's designs. It will go to those who have disciplined themselves, kept the goal in mind, and run to win. In short, it will go to those believers who live the Christian life to the full. Not satisfied with being observers or playing at spirituality, they listen intently to what God wants. Then they draw on his many resources and carry out the work they have been saved to do.

Paul was called, commissioned by the Lord to preach the gospel to the unevangelized, to start churches in areas where no one had preached before and where the Christian population was nil or very small. He was sent to bring the good news of salvation to Jews and Gentiles alike. As Paul said, "It has always been my ambition to preach the gospel where Christ was not known, so that I would not be building on someone else's foundation" (Rom 15:20). That's exactly what he did.

How committed was Paul to accomplish the task God had given him? I'll let him tell you:

> Though I am free and belong to no man, I make myself a slave to everyone, to win as many as possible. To the Jews I became like a Jew, to win the Jews. To those under the law I became like one under the law (though I myself am not under the law), so as to win those under the law. To those not having the law I became like one not having the law (though I am not free from God's law but am under Christ's law), so as to win those not having the law. To the weak I became weak, to win the weak. I have become all things to all men so that by all possible means I might save some. I do all this for the sake of the gospel, that I may share in its blessings.   1 CORINTHIANS 9:19-23

Paul was committed to running his race all out. He gave it everything he had, drawing on all available resources, especially those coming from the Lord, his Word, and his church (see Romans 16; Philippians 4:10-20; 2 Timothy 3:16-17).

Did the effort pay off? Yes. The Christian faith was firmly planted in the Middle East, Asia Minor, and Europe. Thousands upon thousands of people heard the gospel and responded in faith. Skeptics were either converted or silenced. Enemies of the cross became friends of Christ. The sick and disabled were healed. Some were even raised from the dead. The despairing found hope, the depressed found joy. The addicted and chained were freed. The greedy became givers. In short, Paul showed sinners Jesus, and they embraced the Savior in droves (see Acts 9-28).

Paul's efforts were not flawless, nor did they always achieve their mark, as he himself readily acknowledged (Philippians 3:12-14). Despite this, he never stopped running the race God had commissioned him to run. He kept training and racing faithfully.

He even "strain[ed] toward what is ahead" and "press[ed] on toward the goal to win the prize for which God has called [him] me heavenward in Christ Jesus" (vv. 13-14). What Jerry Bridges says about Paul is true: "Paul never had an off season; he never slacked off in his efforts. [His] was a lifelong discipline."[2]

Because of his diligence, toward the end of his days Paul could tell his protégé Timothy, "I have fought the good fight, I have finished the race, I have kept the faith. Now there is in store for me the crown of righteousness, which the Lord, the righteous Judge, will award to me" (2 Tim 4:7-8). Paul ran to win, and he had the resulting confidence that the victory was his. He was already looking forward to his reward.

The Energizer

If you're like me, even on paper this business of "running the race" of the Christian life sounds exhausting. I have deadlines to meet, kids to cart here and there, business meetings to attend, personal and family problems to resolve, hurt feelings to soothe, frustrations to overcome... and on

> We Christians may be very disciplined and industrious in our business, our studies, our home, or even our ministry, but we tend to be lazy when it comes to exercise in our own spiritual lives. We would much rather pray, "Lord, make me godly," and expect him to "pour" some godliness into our souls in some mysterious way. God does in fact work in a mysterious way to make us godly, but he does not do this apart from the fulfillment of our own personal responsibility. We are to train ourselves to be godly.[3]
>
> Jerry Bridges

the list goes. I do not lack for things to do. If anything, I'm looking for things to unload. And then someone comes along and says I'm not doing enough to lead the life God desires. Are you kidding? What more can I do? When am I supposed to find time to do it? And where can I find the energy?

Let's get real. Most Christians today work longer hours than their recent predecessors, struggle to make ends meet financially, face a religiously hostile cultural environment, and have to expend so much time and energy just to live that the goal of spiritual discipline seems unreachable and unreasonable. The entire endeavor appears doomed before it ever starts.

At one time in my life, I felt all these things, and allowed them to cripple my progress toward spiritual maturity. I went forward weakly. But I eventually found out that the disciplined Christian life is liberating and much easier to live than the life I had been trying to lead. I discovered that what Jesus said is absolutely true: "Come to me, all you who are weary and burdened, and I will give you rest. Take my yoke upon you and learn from me, for I am gentle and humble in heart, and you will find rest for your souls. For my yoke is easy and my burden is light" (Mt 11:28-30).

The Christian life is work, but it's much easier to live it the way God intended. *All out!* To be successful, we can't pick and choose what we want to do, when we want to do it, and the manner in which we choose to do it.

If you decided to get in physical shape by running just on Sundays, you'd be kidding yourself. You'd simply run yourself into the ground. Each Sunday you would strain under-used muscles and before long you'd drive your body into a state of exhaustion. If you kept it up, instead of helping your body you'd probably damage it. But if you ran several days a week and exercised according to a workout plan that was progressively more strenuous, you'd be increasing your energy level, and you'd be far less tired. Your everyday life would become easier to tackle, not harder.

That's the way it is with the disciplined Christian life. The spiritual disciplines are part of a divinely sanctioned training program that gradually turns flabby, easily exhausted individuals into finely-tuned, lean, energized people capable of accomplishing spiritual good far beyond their natural abilities. Through the disciplines you will discover ways to ease the weight of pressing burdens and even rid yourself of many of them.

You will find peace, even in the midst of life's storms. Fear will give way to courage. The joy of service will replace the guarded, unsatisfied preoccupation with self. Broken hearts will find genuine comfort and healing. Life will begin to make sense and reveal purpose. The benefits of the disciplined life are innumerable and immeasurable.

The only question is do you want these benefits enough to work for them? If not, you will never know how easy and restful Jesus' yoke can be. You will only know how stressful and unfulfilling your yoke is.

I learned about discipline even before I became a Christian. From my early childhood years, my parents attempted to instill the value of disciplined living into my psyche. They made sure I did my weekly chores, completed all my school homework well and on time, fulfilled the responsibilities of part-time employment, and met and enjoyed the rigors of several other extracurricular activities. It was a valuable beginning. While what they did helped me understand and appreciate a disciplined lifestyle, it was a junior high track coach who burned discipline into my life like a tattoo. He showed me what remarkable feats could be accomplished and enjoyed when discipline's demands are met.

My Story: The Winning Edge

I was in seventh grade and in love with music, history, and girls (not necessarily in that order). I liked nice clothes and combing my hair onto my forehead in a Beach Boys style. I was also enjoying my recent growth spurt that took me from about a five-foot tall blimp to a five-foot, six-inch slender and energetic twelve-year-old. The last thing I wanted to do was drip with sweat and gasp for air on a track with a bunch of other aching guys. Our school track coach, however, saw my future differently.

I was one of about forty other pimply-faced boys in Coach Thornton's gym class. As part of our grade in physical education, we had to run a 330-yard dash against the clock. When my turn came, I burst off the starting line and within a hundred yards left the other runners behind. By the time I crossed the finish line, I had broken the school record for the 330.

I had never run like that before. I had never been able to prior to my growth spurt. In elementary school I used to get back at kids who teased me about my weight by threatening to sit on them. The unfortunate ones who got caught under my gravity-revenge program passed the word that the experience was better left imagined. At that weight, the only sport I excelled at was baseball. I could hit a ball farther than anyone in the entire school. That's because I had more belly power behind the swing.

That day, however, when Coach Thornton saw my race time, he pulled me aside and told me how fast I had run. Since I had nothing to compare it to, I was unimpressed. The achievement was simply lost on me.

It wasn't lost on him, however. He told me he wanted me to come out and practice with the track team the next day. I answered with an unequivocal no. Not to be beat, he calmly assured me that he would flunk me in gym if I didn't have a very short haircut and my carcass on the track field after school the following day. I believed him.

I went home and told my parents what had happened. Even though they probably knew that Coach Thornton would not carry through with his "threat," they believed a busy boy was less likely to do something destructive. So they, too, encouraged me to go out for track. The next day, I had something very close to a

Marine haircut and reported for track where I worked out with long-distance runners.

My first year in track was miserable. I ran two miles and they seemed like ten. All season I worked out long and hard after school five days a week. I even ran in the early morning hours delivering newspapers door to door so I could get in more practice. I tried and tried to win, but no matter how hard I tried, I always finished last or next to last. I came to despise track. I thought I was a failure. Coach Thornton didn't. He knew better. He kept telling me that I could run and that one day my competitors would only see my back in a race. All he asked was that I trust him. I did.

In my second year of track, I finally began to see the payoff. Coach Thornton took me off the long-distance running team and put me with the short-distance runners, then finally with the sprinters. I began working on running dashes. Compared to covering two miles in a race, running a few hundred yards was a breeze. When the other sprinters were wearing out in a race, I was coming on even stronger. The only thing I had any real trouble with was coming out of the starting blocks as quickly as the other runners. Coach Thornton had a cure for that. It was the same cure he had for just about every other malady a runner had. Practice. Practice. Practice. Then practice some more.

My typical workout was rigorous. First calisthenics, then a one-mile jog with the long-distance runners. Next I joined the sprinters for more warmup exercises, drills, and timed dashes against the other sprinters. We did anywhere from six to a dozen of these races each practice. We had three minutes to rest between races. Finally, when most of the sprinters left the field, the coach had me strap five-pound weights around my ankles and a fifteen-pound weight around my chest. Then, carrying all this weight, he had me run six 660-yard dashes allowing only two minutes of rest between them. There was a lot more than this to the training and discipline, and all of it was intense and designed to get the most out of me for the races to come.

At most track meets, I ran three races, the 100-yard dash, 330-yard dash, and 440-yard dash, and usually came in second or third. By the time my third running year came along, I almost always took first place in the 220, 330, and 440 races, and I occasionally set new records. I had strengthened my muscles, developed my lungs, and increased my determination to win the race. Now track was no longer hard work, it was fun.

The Christian's Training Program
A Busy Believer's Guide

Practice	Discipline	Perseverance
Listening	Trusting	Obeying
Focus	Experience	Teamwork

These were the trilogies of success I learned from Coach Thornton and my days in track. I had no idea then that they were also the keys to spiritual growth. It took years of watching, studying, praying, trial and error, and shedding my ideas about what spiritual life is supposed to be before I finally figured it out. This book, *The Busy Christian's Guide to the Deeper Life*, presents some of what I have learned along the way. I have designed it as a beginner's training manual to equip you to finish and win the race of the Christian life. This program will not add to your burdens or exhaust you. It has been set up to ease you into the disciplined Christian life and show you how that life can bring you needed rest and peace even in the midst of life's stresses.

This training program consists of the finest training tools around—the spiritual disciplines. The spiritual disciplines are not the essence of Christianity; Jesus Christ is. Neither are the disciplines the focus of the Christian life; transformation from sinner to saint in Christ is. The disciplines are, however, the means to knowing Christ more fully and to undergoing an abiding, comprehensive transformation. They are time-proven aids in our spiritual journey. They are guides to the deeper Christian life, to a richer experience with God, his creation, and his family called the church. In short, the spiritual disciplines are designed to help us become, through God's enabling grace, the kind of human beings he has created and saved us to be.

As Dallas Willard has said in his insightful book *The Spirit of the Disciplines*, "The disciplines are activities of mind and body purposefully undertaken, to bring our personality and total being into effective cooperation with the divine order. They enable us more and more to live in a power that is, strictly speaking, beyond us, deriving from the spiritual realm itself, as we 'yield ourselves to God, as those that are alive from the dead, and our members as instruments of righteousness unto God,' as Romans 6:13 puts it."[4]

How to Use this Guide

There are many spiritual disciplines. Each discipline, when learned, brings a facet of who we are and what we do into conformity with God's best will for us. While there are many disciplines, in this book I have chosen to cover only six. They are:

- prayer
- study
- journaling
- fasting
- service
- confession

Each discipline is covered in one chapter of the book, and each chapter contains material covering a two-week period. At the beginning of each week you will find introductory material which gives the heart of the lesson about the discipline and explains why it is important for your spiritual development. But this book is not for reading only. It contains exercises for working your spiritual muscles so you can get in better shape to run the race of the Christian life. The introductory material for each week is followed by two days of practical involvement exercises related to that discipline. The weeks are numbered consecutively and so are the exercises. It looks like this:

Week 1	Week 2	Week 3 — And so on.
Day 1	Day 3	Day 5
Day 2	Day 4	Day 6

In other words, in a twelve-week span, you will have twenty-four days worth of exercises.

If you want more out of your walk with God, and I'm assuming you do, then you will be willing to do something more than just read about growing in Christ. In this book you have the opportunity to gain a *working* knowledge of the deeper Christian life. Here is practical, real-world guidance that recognizes you are already too busy and that the idea of adding one more thing to your day seems overwhelming.

What You Will Find

Here's how the book is laid out.

Every two weeks you'll be introduced to a different spiritual discipline, so that by the time twelve weeks have passed, you will have worked through six disciplines. Moreover, you will have practiced each discipline several times, in some cases even before you come to the chapter that concentrates on that discipline.

You see, you don't have to know a lot about a spiritual discipline to begin practicing it. You don't even have to know its name. That's why, for example, you will practice the discipline of study a few times before you get to the chapter that focuses on study.

The chart below shows you the disciplines that are in each chapter. Since each discipline is practiced several times over the twelve weeks of this workbook, you can see that you will have plenty of opportunities to practice all of them and see how they work together to nurture your life with God.

Chapters:	1	2	3	4	5	6
Prayer	✓	✓	✓	✓	✓	✓
Study	✓	✓	✓	✓	✓	✓
Journaling	✓		✓	✓	✓	✓
Fasting				✓	✓	✓
Service			✓	✓	✓	✓
Confession	✓			✓		✓

All you have to do to get the most out of this book is to set aside thirty minutes or less two days a week for twelve weeks to cover the material in this book. That's a maximum one-hour commitment each week for three months. As I'll explain shortly, the book is designed so you can increase this weekly commitment or even decrease it, depending on your schedule, needs, and desires. I can promise you that if you give this small amount of time to developing your spiritual life, in three months you will be a different person—more committed, open, honest, energetic, and more at peace with God and in relationships with other people.

There are two sections in most chapters of the book, and some have three. They are:

✐ Getting Started

This section occurs each day. Its explanations and exercises are basic and important to understanding, appreciating, and practicing the discipline under discussion. For that reason, this is the one section you are encouraged to cover without fail. Doing so will normally take you thirty minutes or less.

▼ Going Deeper *[Optional]*

This section occurs almost every day. As its name suggests, it provides exercises that will take you deeper into the practice of the disciplines. It's an optional section designed for those people who have more time, energy, and desire to make the disciplines a vital part of their life. It can be done on the same day as you do the "Getting Started" section or later in the week.

✓ Checking In

This section appears sporadically throughout the book. It will sometimes remind you of some previous assignment or will ask how you are doing in your practice of the disciplines. Sometimes this section will simply encourage you.

Variety and Flexibility

This interactive resource can be arranged to fit your situation. For instance, you could study one discipline each week and spread out the interactive material to cover five days. For instance:

First day of each week—read the introductory material.

Second day—do the exercises in the first "Getting Started."

Third day—work through the "Going Deeper" section.

Fourth day—do the next "Getting Started" section.

Fifth day—do the next "Going Deeper" section.

Another option would be to skip all the "Going Deeper" sections and simply delve into the "Getting Started" material. You could do one "Getting Started" a week, two a week, three a week, or four or five a week. After you have covered the entire book, you could go back and pick up all the "Going Deeper" sections or zero in on just the ones that strike your interest.

If your current schedule is especially busy, you might want to consider this idea: Set aside ten to fifteen minutes every day or every other day. During that time, give your attention to covering whatever material you can. If all you can do is read that week's introduction, do just that. During the next study time, pick up where you left off. It may take you two weeks or more to work through one week's material. That's OK. The main thing is that you get started and persevere to the end, whatever length of time it takes.

It is possible to work through the entire book in one month or spread out the work over half a year or even longer. The choice is yours and the options are many. There is simply no right or wrong way to work through this book.

I would, however, urge you to do your best to establish a regular weekly schedule. Becoming a disciplined Christian requires developing good habits. Actions cannot become habits without being practiced regularly. This is as true in the spiritual life as it is in every other arena of life. This book will show you how to discipline your life, but it cannot make you a disciplined person. Only you, with the Lord's help, can do that.

At the same time, I ask you to give yourself some flexibility. Life is messy and unpredictable. No matter how well we plan, circumstances have a way of turning our plans into rubble. If that happens to you, give yourself some time to regroup and possibly revise your strategy. Then start moving ahead again. Remember, perseverance is a virtue, and it is a key to attaining spiritual transformation. So don't let some thwarted plans stop you from growing spiritually by God's grace. Strive to maintain a long obedience in the same direction, and God will reward you with a changed life and a crown of righteousness.

Bountiful Benefits

In time and with persistent, prayerful obedience, the spiritual disciplines will move from being an addendum to your life to being as normal as breathing. You will still have daily quiet times with the Lord. Nonetheless, they will be but a small part of your moment-by-moment realization of his presence in your life. You will exude his handiwork, not perfectly but clearly. You will take ready comfort in his presence and know deep, inward joy in doing his works. All will not be bliss—that's reserved for heaven. Still, you will have tasted enough of heaven to know that what awaits you is an eternal glory far surpassing our wildest imaginations. In that state of everlasting bliss we will see Beauty, Truth, Justice, Mercy, Faithfulness, Goodness, Love... all that God is... face to face, summed up and magnified in him infinitely and perfectly. Indeed, we will not only see it but be wrapped in it. Our garments will be divine.

You see, the Lord is not only our Coach but also our Tailor. He has fitted us with the richest clothing of all—the royal raiments of the Father's Son, Jesus Christ, who is truly God and truly man. All a human being was created to be he was in splendid fullness. The perfect visible image of the invisible God—that was Jesus Christ (Colossians 1:15). He is our clothing, but we are not automatically draped in him. We must put him on ourselves. This begins when we trust in Christ "through faith" and are "baptized into Christ" (Galatians 3:26-27). Through these acts we clothe ourselves with him, but we are not to stop here. Our baptism into Christ begins a clothing process that continues throughout our pilgrimage on earth and is consummated in our purified heavenly state. We are to "put aside the deeds of darkness" and "not think about how to gratify the desires of the sinful nature." Instead we are to "clothe [ourselves] with the Lord Jesus Christ" (Rom 13:12, 14). We are called to "put off [our] old self, which is being corrupted by its deceitful desires" and to "put on the new self, created to be like God in true righteousness and holiness." This includes putting off falsehood and speaking truthfully; dealing with anger before it turns into sin; working for a living rather than stealing; building up others according to their needs instead of tearing them down with our words; getting "rid of all bitterness, rage and anger, brawling and slander, along with every form of malice," and replacing these with kindness and compassion and a forgiving spirit as limitless as God's forgiveness of us in Christ (Ephesians 4:22-32). In other words, clothing ourselves with Christ means becoming like him. It means becoming "imitators of God" and living "a life of love, just as Christ loved us and gave himself up for us as a fragrant offering and sacrifice to God" (Eph 5:1-2).

> When sinners become Christians, they receive a new spiritual wardrobe from their heavenly Father (Luke 15:22-24; 2 Corinthians 5:17). But many seem satisfied to walk around in their old clothes in spite of the dirt and grime. They have to be reminded time and again to get rid of the old clothes and put on the new attire God has provided.[5]
>
> Rick Yohn

On our own, this life is completely impossible to live. Clothed with Christ and empowered by his Spirit, this life can be lived. And it is not a burden but a joy—a joy inexpressible and a peace unimaginable.

The clothes are ready to wear. The spiritual disciplines will show you how to wear them so God will be well pleased and you will know his pleasure.

WEEK 1

Connecting with God

"Lord, teach us to pray" (Lk 11:1). The disciples had often watched their Master go off alone to pray. They had heard him pray in their midst when the crowds were not around. And they had seen him pray in public, even when throngs of people were pressing in on him. They knew his prayers produced results—demons fled, blind men regained their sight, diseases disappeared, the dead rose, water became wine, the winds and seas bowed in obedience, the wisdom of the worldly was stripped of its foolishness. God was with this man, in this man, somehow, inexplicably, was this man. And yet, the disciples knew that prayer provided an essential link between the world they could not see and the world they trafficked in day in and day out.

"Lord, teach us to pray. Help us tap into the resources you do. Show us how we can have an intimate, vital relationship with our Creator and Father, as you obviously do." This is what the disciples wanted. This is what every follower of Jesus Christ desires. This is what he wants for his followers.

This week we will look at the discipline of prayer and begin integrating it into our lives. You will discover that learning to pray and seeing benefit from prayer is a process. No relationship deepens overnight. Intimacy and vibrancy take time, patience, constancy, and, perhaps most of all, a committed desire for these attributes to root deeply into the soul and bear spiritual fruit. Nevertheless, all this begins one prayer at a time.

> Prayer is the central avenue God uses to transform us…. The closer we come to the heartbeat of God the more we see our need and the more we desire to be conformed to Christ.[1]
>
> Richard Foster

Before we go any further, let's look at what prayer is. No single definition can exhaust the many sides of prayer. Like a multifaceted jewel, the essence of prayer glimmers in different ways depending on how it reflects the Light. But if we could examine the jewel long enough to see what all of its facets have in common, we would find that the common link within the jewel of prayer is *communion with God*. Like no other spiritual discipline, prayer ushers us into the very presence of the three Persons who are God—the Father, the Son, and the Holy Spirit. Through prayer, we are joined to eternal Love—the Father as the Lover, the Son as the Loved One, and the Holy Spirit as the Bond of Love. We come into the everlasting, harmonious, heavenly Family, the Family which will never abandon or fail us (2 Timothy 2:13; Hebrews 13:5-6).

This is not to say that prayer is easy or always delivers warm fuzzies. In fact, prayer can be hard work, and it can leave us emotionally unmoved. Over time, however, prayer changes lives, not only ours, but also the lives of those for whom we pray. Prayer is the greatest transforming activity in which we can ever engage.

Now, let's get started practicing the discipline of prayer. There's no better place for Christ-followers to start than with the prayer life of Jesus Christ himself.

DAY ONE

✍ Getting Started

1. The passages that follow provide a glimpse into Jesus' practice of prayer. Look up each reference and record what you find about his prayer life. Try to answer the questions under each passage below:

Luke 3:2-3, 21-22
a. Who prayed? _____
b. Where (location) and when (time of day) did the prayer take place? _____
c. Was anyone else around during the prayer time? _____
d. What was the prayer about? (Hint: If the passage does not specify the prayer's subject or exact content, observe what the prayer says or does after praying. The words and actions of the person praying may give you some clues about his prayer.) _____
e. What happened during or after the prayer? _____
_____
_____
f. Who was affected by the prayer? _____
_____

Mark 1:35-39
a. Who prayed? _____
b. Where and when did the prayer take place? _____
c. Was anyone else around during the prayer time? _____
_____
d. What was the prayer about? _____
_____

e. What happened during or after the prayer? _____
_____

f. Who was affected by the prayer? _____
_____

Luke 6:12-16

a. Who prayed? _____

b. Where and when did the prayer take place? _____
_____

c. Was anyone else around during the prayer time? _____
_____

d. What was the prayer about? _____
_____

e. What happened during or after the prayer? _____
_____
_____

f. Who was affected by the prayer? _____
_____

2. Although there are many places where Jesus' words of prayer are recorded, none of the above passages cite his words. Instead, they mention and imply other aspects of his prayer life. For example, did you notice how much Jesus would go off by himself to pray?

What place of solitude can you go to regularly to pray? Is there a room in your home where you can put up a "Do not disturb" sign? A place in your yard or neighborhood you can retreat to? A nearby park? A chapel or church? It doesn't have to be the same place every time, but, if possible, you should try to find a place you can frequent that will give you some uninterrupted time alone with God.

Consider three places you can regularly go to pray, then try praying in each location this week to see which ones fit your needs the best. Don't concern yourself too much with what you pray or how long you pray. Right now the goal is to find one or more places where you can pray regularly and with as few interruptions or distractions as possible. Use this trial process to help you choose the place or places that will work well for you in the weeks ahead. Record your findings here.

The *first* place I chose and how it fit with my needs:

_____

The *second* place I chose and how it fit with my needs:

_____

The *third* place I chose and how it fit with my needs:

_____

 # Going Deeper

Did you notice in this week's Bible passages that Jesus spent a lot of time praying in natural surroundings? He loved the mountains, hills, and valleys. He liked to pray in environments that displayed the Father's handiwork.

Try to get away to a place this week that shows little of what humans have made but much of what God has created. As you look upon it, read aloud Psalms 8 and 19. Ponder God's greatness, power, infinite understanding, and incredible creativity. Raise your voice to God in prayer, allowing him and his creation to motivate your praise, your petitions, your confessions, your thanksgiving. Then linger as long as you can. Let the scene etch itself in your mind and water your soul.

DAY TWO

✍ Getting Started

There are many misperceptions about prayer. You may have heard people say that you must pray a certain way or about certain things, otherwise your prayers will not be effective. That's simply not true. What the Bible reveals is that the life of prayer is as diverse as life itself. Here are a few biblical facts about prayer that even a one-time reading of Scripture clearly conveys:

- *There are no right prayer formulas.* Prayer can be a simple petition, a long praise, a brief thank you, a cry of pain, or a combination of intercessory requests, worshipful proclamations, and even singing.

- *There are no right prayer positions.* You can sit in a chair or on the ground or in a boat, bend one knee or both knees, stand straight or slump, lay face up or prostrate, keep your eyes open or close them, raise your hands upward, or cross them in front of you or behind you, or leave them dangling at your side.

- *There are no right prayer words.* The prayers in Scripture are as varied as human experience and emotion. Some prayers call for judgment, others for mercy. Other prayers are filled with anger, while many express deep remorse. Some prayers praise God for hard fought victories, as other prayers ask for his help in unexpected defeat.

- *There are no right prayer places.* Prayers are offered to God on battlefields; on quiet, grassy hillsides; beside refreshing streams; next to dried-up river beds, in cities, fortresses, and country homes, on the job site; in deserts; on the high seas; and, in one prophet's case, in the belly of a great sea creature (see Jonah 2).

- *There are no right prayer times.* You can pray any time of day or night. Prayer can last just seconds, minutes, hours, or even days. And prayer can be offered on any occasion and during any circumstance.

- *There are no right prayer feelings or thoughts.* Prayer can communicate anger and pain, joy and sorrow, reasonableness and illogic, understanding and confusion, hate and love, wisdom and foolishness, faith and doubt.

In short, nothing is off limits in prayer. God can take anything we dish out, anywhere, anytime, in any position we wish to deliver it. He knows us better than we know ourselves anyway. He knows our feelings and our thoughts even if we never articulate them to him. We cannot keep anything from him (Psalms 139:1-4; Hebrews 4:13). So why should we try? We don't have to sugarcoat our hurt or cover up our anger or deny our faithlessness or hide our dishonesty. God is the one Person we can tell everything to and know we are accepted no matter what. He loves us in Christ unconditionally (Romans 8:31-39). We can never find a better deal than that.

1. With these facts in mind, let's look again at Jesus and his prayer life. Read the passages listed below, looking for answers to the same six questions posed in "Day One":

Luke 9:28-36
a. Who prayed? _____
b. Where and when did the prayer take place? _____

_____

c. Was anyone else around during the prayer time? _____

_____

d. What was the prayer about? _____

_____

e. What happened during or after the prayer? _____

_____

f. Who was affected by the prayer? _____

_____

Mark 8:1-10

a. Who prayed? _____

b. Where (location) and when (time of day) did the prayer take place? _____

c. Was anyone else around during the prayer time? _____

_____

d. What was the prayer about? _____

_____

e. What happened during or after the prayer? _____

_____

f. Who was affected by the prayer? _____

_____

2. The Bible passages you have explored so far show times in which Jesus prayed alone in the early morning hours or later at night. One of the texts shows him offering a prayer of gratitude during the day in front of a hungry crowd of searchers.

Like Jesus, we can pray anytime, anywhere, before anyone. However, if we want to really develop our prayer life to its greatest potential, we need to find a time of day that will afford us real quiet time before God. Again, the time of day we choose (morning, afternoon, or evening) may fluctuate, but we should pray consistently, preferably daily. On some days our prayer time may be only minutes. As you'll see, the length of time is not nearly as important as the regularity.

Think about times this week you can set aside for prayer. Schedule the time, then guard it jealously. If interruptions occur that demand your time, don't let that frustrate or anger you. Take care of the demand, then set aside another time, the same day if possible, when you can come before God alone in prayer.

> You'll never find time to pray.... You have to make time to pray. It takes sacrifice.
> Something has to go, usually something that seems important.[2]
>
> Peter Kreeft

3. Now take the rest of today's time and pray. Remember, there's no right way to pray, no right words to say, no right emotions or thoughts you must convey. Just turn your mind and heart to God and talk to him. Share yourself with him. Tell him about your concerns, your hurts, your sins, your hopes, your dreams. Ask him to show himself to you. Let him begin to change you and your world through the transforming power of prayer.

Going Deeper

This week you have seen that Jesus prayed alone and he also prayed in the presence of other people. He knew he needed to pray privately, but he also knew that sometimes his prayers needed to be public.

You have spent a fair amount of time this week praying alone. How about taking advantage of an opportunity to pray before others? You might choose to offer God thanks for a meal with your family, friends, or coworkers present. Or you might decide to pray with someone who is depressed, ill, or has another type of need. Maybe you have a son or a daughter with whom you can pray. Or perhaps you can find an opportunity at church to lift up your voice to the Lord. Look for an occasion you can practice publicly what you have been doing privately.

Remember, your prayer can be brief, and it does not have to reveal a personal need unless that is what you want. The goal of this exercise is simply to help you move out from your prayer closet and into the larger world. As you will discover, the spiritual disciplines need to be cultivated privately *and* publicly, and their benefits always reach beyond the individual practitioner.

WEEK 2

Attitudes and Answers

"When I pray nothing happens," she said with a trace of anger and desperation.

"What do you mean 'nothing happens'?" I asked.

"I mean I get no response. I might as well be talking to myself." Her eyes penetrated mine as she spoke. Then, with her point made, she looked away, the corners of her mouth bent downward.

"Let me see if I understand you," I said somewhat slowly and cautiously. "You come before God in prayer and ask him for something or share something with him, but all you get in return is stony silence. He says nothing. He does nothing. And nothing happens in your life to indicate in any way that God heard your prayer."

Without turning her face back toward me, she defiantly answered, "That's right. That's what I'm saying. I pour my heart out to him, but he does nothing in return. It's a one-way street relationship that dead ends."

"Hmm. That puzzles me," I responded, looking off into the distance. "You mean that when you pray you never walk away feeling better about the situation? You never have a better idea what to do? You never hear a still, small voice pointing you in a certain direction? You mean you never find yourself more sensitive to another person's needs? None of these things ever happens to you?"

She moved her head back in my direction and gazed at me with a quizzical look. "Well, yeah, I've had things like that occur."

"Then," I quickly said, "you've received answers to your prayers."

"Those are answers?"

"They sure are. What were you expecting?"

She thought for a minute, then answered, "Well, I suppose I expected God to answer my prayers a certain way. You know, I pray for God to heal someone, and he would make the person well again. I ask him to cause my boss to give me a raise, and my next paycheck would show an increase. I expected God to give me what I asked him for."

"So when he didn't deliver according to your expectations, you thought he wasn't answering you. Right?"

"Yeah, I guess so."

Great expectations. We all have them. And when we come to God—the Being who is all-powerful, all-knowing, all-loving, and all-merciful—our expectations soar. And why not? The Bible and church history are filled with stories of God answering his people's prayers, often in dramatic ways. He is the One who heard the Hebrews' prayers and freed them from slavery in Egypt, brought them into the Promised Land, and helped them conquer it (Exodus; Joshua). He is the One who provided his people food from heaven and water from rocks (Exodus 16-17). He is the One who through his Son healed the disabled and sick, freed the oppressed, fed the hungry, forgave sinners, and raised the dead (Matthew 11:2-6; 15:29-38; Luke 4:16-21; John 8:1-12; 11:1-44). All this is true, but it is only part of the story.

For example, Moses, the man God chose to lead the Hebrews out of Egypt, murdered an Egyptian in an attempt to free the slaves in a way God never intended. Consequently, he ended up having to flee Egypt and herd sheep for forty years before he was ready to carry out God's liberation plan (Exodus 2; Acts 7:17-34). Then when God approached Moses with his plan, Moses balked and had to be convinced that the Lord would stand with him every step of the way (Exodus 3:1-4:18).

When Moses returned to Egypt, the Hebrews spurned him as their leader, not just once but several times. He became so depressed and frustrated over the situation that he cried out to God, suggesting his choice of a deliverer was a mistake (Exodus 5:22-23; 6:9, 12). It took ten incredible miracles of judgment to convince the Egyptian Pharaoh to free the Hebrew slaves and to convince the Hebrews that God was indeed liberating them through Moses (Exodus 7-12).

Once the Hebrews were out of Egypt, it didn't take long before their bouts of disbelief in God and Moses, their lapses into idolatry, and their almost constant complaining led God to condemn them to wander for forty years in the desolate regions of what we call the Sinai Peninsula. Only after that period of testing and discipline did he lead them into the Promised Land of ancient Canaan (Numbers 14:11-38).

During Jesus' ministry in first-century Palestine, the situation was just as complex. He certainly worked wonders among the people, but his ways were frequently not compatible with their expectations. For instance, when his close friend Lazarus was gravely ill, Jesus ignored the pleas of Mary and Martha to rush to their brother's side. Only after he learned of Lazarus' death did Jesus begin to travel to his home. Once he got there, Mary and Martha placed the onus of responsibility for Lazarus' death on Jesus. They told him that if he had only come when he first heard about Lazarus' poor condition, he could have saved their brother (John 11:20-21, 32). That's certainly true, but it would not have accomplished what the Father wanted his Son to do, which was to raise Lazarus from the dead in front of many witnesses. In this way Jesus was glorified and heralded as the long-awaited Messiah (John 11:1-4, 11-15, 23-27, 38-45).

In the prophecy of Isaiah, God declares,

> For my thoughts are not your thoughts,
> neither are your ways my ways....
> As the heavens are higher than the earth,
> so are my ways higher than your ways
> and my thoughts than your thoughts.   Isaiah 55:8-9

We must keep this in mind when it comes to prayer. God will always answer our prayers. However, he is not a vending machine. We can't just drop a prayer into the God-slot, make our selection, and expect to get the answer we want when we want it. The Lord just doesn't work that way. He will frequently not answer us the way we expect. His answer may be yes or no, now or later, soon or never. He may respond to us far beyond our wildest imaginations, or he may not give us as much as we want but certainly enough to meet our need. When we pray, we must be ready to accept his answers, his way, and according to his timetable.

Because he always has our best interests at heart and knows us and our situation exhaustively, we can completely trust him to answer our prayers for our good. As the great apostle Paul said centuries ago, "We know that in all things God works for the good of those who love him, who have been called according to his purpose" (Rom 8:28).

Let's return now to the practice of prayer, this time focusing on our attitudes and his answers.

DAY THREE
✍ Getting Started

1. Since God always gives us what is best for us and at the right moment, we should approach our prayer time with certain attitudes. By "attitudes" I mean dispositions of the heart. And by "heart" I do not mean the physical organ but the center of our personal life.

   If someone gives us a precious gift and we accept it as if we deserve it, we display a haughty spirit that comes from deep within us. On the other hand, if we accept such a gift with genuine thankfulness, we show a humility rooted in our self-understanding. Both actions display the dispositions of our heart, our inner selves. Our attitudes are revealed in our actions and reactions. This is because our heart, even more than our mind, reveals who we really are inside. Try as we might, we cannot completely hide our true selves. We may deceive other people for a time, but eventually the truth will come out. Of course, we can never deceive God. He "judges the thoughts and attitudes of the heart. Nothing in all creation is hidden from God's sight. Everything is uncovered and laid bare before the eyes of him to whom we must give account" (Heb 4:12-13).

   Henri Nouwen provides a helpful explanation of the biblical view of the human heart:

   > The word "heart" in the Jewish-Christian tradition refers to the source of all physical, emotional, intellectual, volitional, and moral energies.
   >
   > From the heart arise unknowable impulses as well as conscious feelings, moods, and wishes. The heart, too, has its reasons and is the center of perception and understanding.

Finally, the heart is the seat of the will: it makes plans and comes to… decisions. Thus the heart is the central and unifying organ of our personal life…. It is this heart that is the place of prayer. The prayer of the heart is a prayer that directs itself to God from the center of the person and thus affects the whole of our humanness.[1]

The following Bible passages speak about various attitudes of the heart, sometimes in relationship to prayer, at other times in relationship to other people or God. Read each passage, looking for the attitudes God honors and the ones he disdains. Fill in the chart with your findings.

Scriptures to Consider	Attitudes to Cultivate	Attitudes to Weed Out
Proverbs 6:16-19		
Romans 12:9-18		
Philippians 2:3-4		
Colossians 4:2		

2. Prayerfully review your answers in the chart, asking the Lord to help you cultivate the right attitudes and weed out the others. This is a prayer request he will answer with a resounding yes, because his revealed desire for all his children is that they become pure in heart (Matthew 5:8; Acts 15:8-9; 1 Thessalonians 3:12-13; James 4:8).

This process—and it is a process that takes time and effort—may push you beyond your comfort zone. You may discover some things about yourself that you don't like.

Harder still, you may see some characteristics in yourself that you like but God does not. Be honest with him about your thoughts, feelings, and struggles. Ask him to help you see what changes you need to make and how you can make them. God is in the transformation business. If you really want to change, he will show you how and empower your efforts through the work of the Holy Spirit (Acts 1:8; 4:31; 13:52; Romans 8; 2 Corinthians 3:17-18; Galatians 5:16-26).

You might want to begin the process by zeroing in on two attitudes to cultivate and two to lose. Feel free to use the prayer below to help you commit to the process, and be sure to make these attitudes a matter of prayer over the weeks to come. Keep your mind and heart open to the Spirit's work in your life, for God desires "to present you holy in his sight, without blemish and free from accusation—if you continue in your faith, established and firm, not moved from the hope held out in the gospel" (Col 1:22-23).

With your gracious help, Lord, I commit to developing the heart attitudes of _____ and _____ in my life. I would also like to ask you to help me purge the heart attitudes of _____ and _____. I realize I am entering a process that may be tough at times, but I trust you to be with me, to strengthen me, to work your transforming power within me until you make me into the kind of person you created me to be.

Going Deeper

Self-evaluation can be difficult. We are often blind to some of our faults, even the more irritating and egregious ones. Also, we often do not clearly see what other people find most laudable in us.

Consider getting together with one or two people close to you who will shoot straight with you about what they see as your personal strengths and weaknesses. I would suggest you ask them to begin by listing your strengths. This will make it easier for you to accept what they say about your weaknesses.

Be prepared to be surprised and perhaps even perplexed and troubled. Give these folks plenty of room to share their assessments of you. If you begin to feel overwhelmed, gently end the conversation, thanking the participants for their time and openness. Remember, they may feel nervous about how you will receive their comments. Do your best to make them feel safe and comfortable during and after the conversation.

Then take what they tell you and bring it before God in prayer. Ask him to help you work through the comments made and, if need be, to add to or revise the commitments you made above in light of the new insights gleaned.

DAY FOUR
✍ Getting Started

Different kinds of prayer bring different answers.

- *Intercession* involves praying for the needs of others, so the answer would be met needs.

- *Petition* is concerned with asking God for something, usually for oneself. An answer to a petition would then be receiving what one requested or something God deemed better.

- *Confession* is asking God's forgiveness for sins. Sins are violations of what God deems good and right. The prayer of confession involves admitting to the Lord what we have done wrong and asking him to remove the penalty of our wrongdoing from us. The penalty of sin is always death (Genesis 2:16-17; Romans 6:23). In Scripture "death" means a separation that tears asunder something designed to stay together. For example, the death of a marriage is divorce (Matthew 19:3-9); the death of a friendship is betrayal (Psalms 41:9; 55:12-14); the death of a human being is the separation of the body from the soul (Psalms 104:29; Ecclesiastes 12:5-7). When we confess our sins, we receive God's forgiveness, but this does not mean we will avoid all the consequences of our sins. Some effects of our wrongdoing may go on for a long time (Numbers14:19-38; 2 Samuel 12:1-23).

- *Thanksgiving* is the prayer of gratitude. It focuses on thanking the Lord for who he is or for what he has done, is doing, or will do. The answer to the prayer of thanksgiving is often a deepening of the heart attitude of gratitude. The more we give thanks, the more we become thankful people.

- *Adoration* is worshipful prayer. Through adoration we express our deep reverence for the Lord. He is our focus. He is the One we glorify and herald as the Lord of lords, Ruler of rulers, the First and the Last, the only God, Creator, and Savior. He is the One we uphold as the only One worthy of our complete devotion. An answer to our adoration is a better understanding of our status as creatures. We come to realize that we have power but he is all-powerful, that we have knowledge but he is all-knowing, that we can do some things for ourselves but we cannot do anything apart from him. A proper self-understanding is important in our development into spiritually mature adults. Adoration can help us achieve that goal.

1. What is commonly known as the Lord's Prayer contains elements of many of these kinds of prayer. Jesus gave his disciples this prayer model in response to their request that he teach them how to pray.

This prayer is reprinted below. You will see arrows pointing to phrases or the end of sentences. Beside these arrows, write in the word that best describes what element of prayer has just been uttered. To get you going, I have filled in the word that best describes the kind of prayer wrapped up in the words "Our Father in heaven, Hallowed be your name."

> Our Father in heaven,
> Hallowed be your name. ← *adoration*
> Your kingdom come. ←
> Your will be done
> On earth as it is in heaven. ←
> Give us this day our daily bread. ←
> And forgive us our debts,
> As we forgive our debtors. ←
> And do not lead us into temptation,
> But deliver us from the evil one. ←
> For Yours is the kingdom and
> the power and the glory forever. Amen. ←
>
> MATTHEW 6:9-13, NKJV

2. Now return to the Lord's Prayer and make it your own. Personalize it. Here's what I mean. After you say the first line, you might expand on it by saying something like this: "I am so grateful that you, Lord, are my Father. As my Father you are perfect and unfailing like no earthly parent could ever be. You always seek my best. You always love me. You always discipline me in a way that will make me a more whole human being. May you always be exalted and adored by me and the rest of your creation."

Do what you can to make each line your own as you lift your voice toward heaven in prayer to the Lord. If you come across a line or word you don't understand, that's OK. Tell the Father that you're not sure what that word or line means, and ask him to help you understand it. Then go to the next line and continue your prayer time.

The Scriptures reveal God's thoughts and ways to us, and the Lord's Prayer tells us a great deal about how God wants us to pray. When you take him at his Word and pray his words back to him, you can be assured that he will honor your prayer as he honors his own Word.

Going Deeper

Once an old sister asked St. Teresa: "How can I become a contemplative?" The saint replied: "Say the 'Our Father,' but take an hour to say it." We may not often be able to take an hour to say the Lord's Prayer, but if we really want to learn to pray, it is good occasionally to take time with the Lord's Prayer and let each phrase open out within us and give voice to the deep longings that the Spirit has planted in our hearts.[2]

M. Basil Pennington

Some people like to write their prayers rather than vocalize them. Putting prayers in writing can make it easier to focus our thoughts and feelings and perhaps say some things we find too difficult to speak. It can also give us a record of our growing relationship with the Lord and progress in the faith.

Write out a prayer to God. Pen what comes to mind, what is troubling your heart, what is making you happy or sad. Direct your words to God. Invite his involvement in your private world. If you hear him speak, put that on paper too, then respond to him in writing. Let the great conversation unfold.

WEEK 3

What Lovers Do

He loved his wife. He loved her so much that he set out to learn everything about her he could. He believed the better he knew her, the better he would know how to love her. So he began to study her. It was only then that he learned things about her he may have never discovered otherwise.

He noticed that when she was under a great deal of stress, she would still be kind and considerate to others, but she would clench her fists, often holding them tightly to her side when standing or pressing them into her lap when sitting.

When she was afraid or nervous, he found she withdrew from him. However, he learned that she didn't want him to pull away from her. On the contrary, she wanted him to come closer, to hold her quietly and firmly, to help her feel safe.

He had often told her that he loved her, but as he studied her he came to realize that she needed so much more. So he began to bring her surprise gifts—a stuffed Winnie the Pooh bear, roses and sunflowers, compact discs of her favorite artists, perfume, tickets to concerts and plays, and such. He started to take her hand, raise it to his lips, gently kiss it, and softly tell her how precious she was in his sight. He went on long walks with her at her favorite getaway spots. He accompanied her to some movies she really wanted to see.

For the first time in their marriage, he noticed that she rarely shared with him from her heart, and on those few times when she did, she would often shut down fairly quickly. After critically reflecting on the incidents, he soon came to see that he was part of the problem. She wanted someone to talk to; he was looking for a problem to solve. She wanted to share her feelings and thoughts; he wanted to analyze them and show her where she was "illogical" or being "ridiculous." So he started to change the way he related to her. He listened to her more with his heart. He asked more questions seeking understanding, leaving behind words that bespoke criticism. He became more intent on coming alongside her rather than instructing her.

The more he learned about her, the more he came to appreciate her. He began to see her as a woman of great depth and strength. He saw her courage, her ability to overcome her fears and act for her own good as well as the good of others. He saw how much she gave to those she loved and how much more she could achieve with the proper support and encouragement. He also noticed some weaknesses he had never seen before. He saw how her physical reaction to stress was tearing down her body and how her tendency to withdraw from people when afraid often left her feeling alone and abandoned.

After just a year of studying his wife, he wrote in his journal:

I have married a woman I didn't really know until now. She's not the woman I thought I had married. She's so much better, richer, real, alive. I can truly say that I love her more now than I ever have. I am anxious to learn even more about this beautiful, mysterious creature I call my wife.

I have also found that my learning experience has changed me. I am not the man my wife married. I have grown. I understand more, notice more, appreciate more, and love more deeply than I ever have at anytime in my life. I have also come to see my own strengths and weaknesses, in some cases for the very first time, and in almost all cases more clearly and realistically than ever. My study has certainly enriched me as a person and as a lover. I would never have imagined that becoming so focused on someone else would have benefited me so much.

The best lovers are the best students of those they love. They are so struck by the objects of their passion that they devote themselves to learning all they can about them. Their desire is to please them, to grant their wishes and satisfy their needs. They want all the best for their loved ones, so they seek to learn what will benefit their loved ones the most: then they strive to meet the need. In the process, the students change and their ability to love expands and matures. Study can be a very loving act for lover and loved one alike.

The spiritual discipline of study is also an act of love. Two millennia ago, Jesus echoed the words of Moses and said that the greatest commandment was, "Love the Lord your God with all your heart and with all your soul and with all your mind." The second greatest commandment, which he said was like the first, was to "Love your neighbor as yourself" (Mt 22:37, 39). Love requires study. You cannot love what you do not know. And you cannot love deeply what you know superficially. If we are going to love God with our whole being, which is what the greatest commandment calls us to do, we must come to really know him. And if we are going to love our neighbor as we do ourselves, like the husband who studied his wife, we must become students of our neighbors. The more we study God and our fellow human beings, the more we will learn about ourselves, and the more our love for them and ourselves will grow.

> God loves us; not because we are loveable but because He is love, not because He needs to receive but because He delights to give.[1]
>
> God, who needs nothing, loves into existence wholly superfluous creatures in order that He may love and perfect them.[2]
>
> C. S. Lewis

One critical difference between our love for God and our love for other people is that people need to be loved while God does not. God *is* love (1 John 4:8, 16). His very nature is infinitely rich in love. The Father loves the Son and the Spirit, the Son loves the Father and the Spirit, and the Spirit loves the Father and the Son. Within himself, God is an eternal, superabundant exchange of love. Therefore, he does not need the love of anyone else. We, on the other hand, need to love and be loved in order to find our true fulfillment. It is in the fountain of all love, God himself, that our true fulfillment is found. He calls on us to love him, not because he needs our love but because we need to love him.

To love as we should, we must take up the discipline of study. To love God as we should, we need to study his revelations to us. In the history of the church's reflections on God, Christians have recognized several kinds of revelation:

- *General or natural revelation*, which is the revelation of God coming through the created order, including human nature and human history since human beings have been created as God's image-bearers (Genesis 1:26-28; James 3:9);

- *Special or written revelation*, which is the God-breathed words of the Holy Scriptures (2 Timothy 3:16-17);

- *Personal or living revelation*, which is the culmination of God's revelation in the person and ministry of the Word incarnate—Jesus Christ, the Son of God and Son of Man (John 1:1-4, 14; Hebrews 1:1-4; 1 John 1:1-4);

- *Private or mystical revelation*, which is what God reveals to individuals for their own guidance, development, assurance, or judgment but which is rarely intended for wider use (Daniel 4).

The category of private revelation, while accepted and appreciated in most Christian traditions, is considered illegitimate or suspect in some. The other three forms of revelation, however, have been readily embraced throughout church history and across orthodox confessional spectrums as reliable, trustworthy, and authoritative. In theological discussions on revelation, personal revelation is frequently subsumed under special revelation since what God has told us about Jesus has been set down in the Bible.

So you can get a handle on what the discipline of study involves, we will narrow the focus to the study of Scripture. Keep in mind, though, that many methods used in the study of the Bible can also be applied to the study of natural revelation.

There are three basic steps in the study process: observation, interpretation, and application. This week we will focus on observation. Next week we will get into interpretation. Then, when we delve into the discipline of journaling, we'll also get our feet wet in biblical application.

DAY FIVE

✍🏻 Getting Started

1. Before you go any further, take some moments to pray. Commit your learning time to the Lord. Ask him to help you understand the material and to use it well.

2. *The first step in the study process is observation.* In this step you are looking for an answer to the central question, what do I see? You want to learn what the text says, not what it means or how it might apply to you. You're not trying to interpret the message, just to read it correctly. You're looking for the facts.

    Some facts to search for are these:

    a. *Grammar:* subjects, verbs, objects, prepositions, connectives, adversatives, etc. (There's rarely a need to put a grammatical label on every word in a biblical passage. I recommend doing it with words that appear to play a key role in the passage.)

b. *Terms*: repeated, unusual, or emphasized words and phrases; terms you don't understand or that require clarification; terms contrasted or compared with one another.

c. *Genre*: the kind of literature it is—poetry, parable (fictional story), narrative (historical story), biography, autobiography, dialogue, correspondence, apocalyptic (meaning futuristic or prophetic), satire, tragedy, allegory, comedy, exhortation, explanation, instructional, argumentative (a reasoned argument).

d. *Historical details:* the writer or speaker, the audience, the setting (for example, city or country, indoors or outdoors, a home or a synagogue, peacetime or wartime, Rome or Jerusalem), related events and their order.

e. *Atmosphere*: the mood (happy or sad, angry or fearful), the smells (sweet or foul), the sounds (soothing or grating, whispers or shouts).

f. *Context*: what precedes and what follows the text and how that relates to the text at hand.

This may seem like a lot of things to look for, but the more time you spend discovering the facts of a text, the less time you will need interpreting the text. Observation done well is the key to coming to a sound interpretation. All you have to do to understand how important hearing what's said correctly is to reflect on times when someone has misunderstood you, and you have misunderstood another. We want to hear what our divine Lover says so we won't make mistakes about what he's telling us.

Since you have already looked at the Lord's Prayer a little bit, you can begin exercising your observational muscles on that passage. The prayer is printed below, along with a small portion of its context (Matthew 6:5-15, NKJV). I have made a few observations to help you get started.

You will need more room to jot down your observations

than you will find below. You may want to enlarge the biblical text on a photocopier or reproduce the text another way. I recommend you leave three to five spaces of blank lines between each line of text and that you make the page margins 1-1/2" to 2". This will give you ample room to record your observations.

Give whatever time you have left today to making observations on this biblical passage. Don't worry about completing your work. We're going to return to discovering what this passage says in the next day's exercises.

SPEAKER: *Jesus*

AUDIENCE: *Disciples and the multitudes who followed Jesus from Galilee, Jerusalem, Judea, and beyond the Jordan River (4:25-5:1). Find these places on a map, learn distances, etc.*

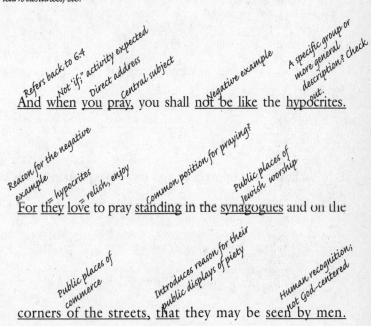

Refers back to 6:4
Not "if;" activity expected
Direct address
Central subject
Negative example
A specific group or more general description? Check out.

And when you pray, you shall not be like the hypocrites.

Reason for the negative example
= hypocrites
= relish, enjoy
common position for praying?
Public places of Jewish worship

For they love to pray standing in the synagogues and on the

Public places of commerce
Introduces reason for their public displays of piety
Human recognition; not God-centered

corners of the streets, that they may be seen by men.

Assuredly, I say to you, they have their reward. But you,

when you pray, go into your room, and when you have shut

your door, pray to your Father who is in the secret place;

and your Father who sees in secret will reward you openly.

But when you pray, do not use vain repetitions as the hea-

then do. For they think that they will be heard for their many words. Therefore do not be like them. For your Father

knows the things you have need of before you ask him.

In this manner, therefore, pray:

Our Father in heaven,

Hallowed be your name.

Your kingdom come.

Your will be done

On earth as it is in heaven.

Give us this day our daily bread.

And forgive us our debts,

As we forgive our debtors.

And do not lead us into temptation,

But deliver us from the evil one.

For yours is the kingdom and

the power and the glory forever. Amen.

For if you forgive men their trespasses, your heavenly

Father will also forgive you. But if you do not forgive

men their trespasses, neither will your Father forgive your

trespasses.

Going Deeper

A good way to notice more in a biblical text is to read it aloud. Do this with the Matthew passage on the Lord's Prayer. See if your ears catch connections and inflections that your eyes missed. Add any new observations to the ones you've made already.

✓ Checking In

Do you recall the heart attitudes you wanted to develop and the ones you wanted to lose? You prayed about these during Week 2, Day 3. Have you continued bringing these before God as a matter of prayer? The Lord wants us to be persistent in our prayers (Luke 18:1-8). Don't let up asking him to help you change for the better.

DAY SIX

✍ Getting Started

1. Open your time in prayer. Take any concerns you have to God. Lay them at the foot of his throne and ask him to help you deal with them. Then, with God's help, settle your mind and heart so you can learn more about the discipline of study.

> The depth of the Christian Scriptures is boundless. Even if I were attempting to study them and nothing else, from boyhood to decrepit old age, with the utmost leisure, the most unwearied zeal, and with talents greater than I possess, I would still be making progress in discovering their treasures.[3]
>
> Augustine

2. Return to the Lord's Prayer passage and study it again. Even if you made it through the whole passage making observations last time, walk through it once more. You'll find yourself noticing things you had missed before.

3. Now summarize your discoveries by completing these statements:

The genre is

_____ .

The speaker is

_____ .

The audience is

_____ .

The setting is _____ .

The events immediately leading up to this passage are

_____ .

The events immediately following this passage are

_____ .

The atmosphere is _____ .

The topic of the text is _____ .

The key words are _____ .

Words to define are _____

_____ .

The context is _____

_____ .

Some other important or interesting observations I made are

_____

_____

_____

_____

_____

Some questions I would like to answer are

_____

_____

_____

_____

_____

4. Close in prayer, thanking the Lord for the guidance he provided as you worked through a portion of his Word today.

Going Deeper

Memorizing Scripture is an excellent way to get God's Word working inside you. It's a way of accomplishing what the psalmist sought to do: "I have hidden your word in my heart that I might not sin against you" (Ps 119:11).

If you have never done so before, try memorizing just the Lord's Prayer (Matthew 6:9-13). It may take you a few days to get it down, but the time you spend doing it will be worthwhile. With the prayer committed to memory, you can pray it any time; you can meditate on its truths more conveniently and frequently; and you can readily apply its truths to situations you can't even imagine right now.

WEEK 4

Seeing Red

When I was a high school student in the late 1960s, my parents surprised me with an incredible Christmas present: they gave me a six-week trip to Europe. The trip was with the Foreign Study League, and its purpose was to tour several European countries while learning about their history, customs, and languages. About 170 high school students, accompanied by nearly twenty adult teachers, went on the tour.

Our first stop was London, England. There we began what would become routine throughout the tour. We spent four or five mornings per week in classroom settings learning about the country and city we were in. In the afternoons and evenings we would get out in our surroundings, visiting important historical sites, sightseeing, shopping, and simply experiencing a new culture firsthand.

Our morning classes were taught by our teacher chaperons, local university students, or on occasion, local professors or government officials. During one of our class sessions in London, a university student came to orient us to the local customs and to advise us on the best places to visit. Before he left, he gave the females in our group a warning. He told them to avoid going out at night wearing a red dress, especially if they were unaccompanied by a man. At that time (I don't know if it's still true), a red dress on a woman getting around London in the evening hours marked her as a prostitute. So if women didn't want to be propositioned, they needed to wear dresses of a color other than red.

That night, one of our teacher chaperons left to attend a play being performed across town. She went out alone, and she wore a red dress. She had not heard the student lecturer's warning.

On her way to the play, she took a taxi and didn't encounter any problems. After the play, she decided to return on London's subway system, which at that time was quite safe to travel any time of day or night. While on the train, she noticed a couple of men leering at her.

When she got off at her stop, one of the men came up to her and began making advances as he would with a woman of the night. Another man joined them and began doing the same.

Understandably, our teacher was confused and afraid, and she tried to put the men straight. But they thought she was just playing hard to get, so they became more direct and vocal about their wishes. At this she turned away from them and began to run. A broken heel, a lost shoe, and two long city blocks later, she managed to convince her pursuers to give up the chase by outrunning them. It wasn't until she got back to our tour group and relayed her awful experience that she learned the color of her dress had been the cause.

This teacher had an encounter with interpretation, even though during the experience she did not understand why it was happening. For her the red dress she wore meant appropriate attire for attending the performance of a play. For London men the red dress meant an evening of sexual play with a performer of a different sort. Different cultures with different customs brought different interpretations to the same object.

The same thing happens when people approach the Bible and attempt to discover its meaning. They interpret it in different ways frequently because they view it through different interpretive glasses. Just as blue-colored glasses give a blue tinge to what a person sees, so different backgrounds influence people to view the same facts differently. Upbringing, local customs, education, profession, religious instruction, beliefs, and a number of other factors will affect the meaning people attach to what they observe or read. What they may see is the same, but what they think it means is not.

Therefore, after we have come to know what a biblical text says, we need to learn what it means by what it says. In other words, *the second step in the study process is to discover what God means by what he has said in his written Word.* The apostle Paul tells us that the Scriptures are "God-breathed" (2 Tim 3:16), which means that God inspired the human writers to put down on parchment what he wanted them to say. He used their talents, their language, their reasoning abilities, and their experience to contextualize and convey his message to humankind. The result is that their words are his words and their message is his message.

So, to understand his message, we need to understand the writers' message. That requires getting to know the biblical writers, their times, their cultures, their customs, their lands, and, to some degree, their languages. We also need to learn about the audiences they sought to reach with their writings. Like the chaperon wearing a red dress, we don't want to go out into the world with one interpretation in mind only to find out, perhaps in an embarrassing or frightening way, that we were wrong.

Once we understand a passage's meaning, we are ready to consider its applications. For "all Scripture," says Paul, "is useful for teaching, rebuking, correcting and training in righteousness, so that the man [or woman] of God may be thoroughly equipped for every good work" (2 Tim 3:16-17). God's Word may be ancient, but it still speaks to our day. *Application, which is the third step in the study process, seeks to discover a text's enduring relevance to contemporary people and their times.*

Of course, a text will likely be misapplied if it has been misinterpreted. Coming to a correct interpretation is critical to arriving at valid applications. So in this week's exercises, we will work on interpretation only. When we cover the discipline of journaling beginning next week, we will spend time on application.

DAY SEVEN

✍ Getting Started

In today's lesson, I want you to get a handle on what interpretation is and what it involves when applied to Scripture. You will apply what you learn here in the following day's exercises. So today, just strive to read with understanding. Ask God to aid you before you begin.

1. **What is interpretation?** The step of interpretation seeks to answer the central question, what does the text mean? *You're not trying to determine what the text means to you.* You want to get at what the writer meant by what he wrote. For example, someone who rejects the possibility of miracles might interpret the biblical accounts of Jesus' resurrection as mythical stories intended to inspire us to persevere even through the toughest forms of adversity. For when we do, we will find that, like Jesus, we will rise to the top as stronger, better persons and finally receive the recognition we deserve. This is interpreting the Bible according to what it means to the interpreter, but there is another way to interpret Scripture.

   To the human authors who wrote about Jesus rising alive from the grave, the Resurrection was historical proof that Jesus was the Son of God incarnate, the prophesied Messiah, the victorious Savior of the world (Luke 24:45-49; John 20:19-31; Acts 2:22-36, 17:31-32; 1 Corinthians 15:1-28). This second interpretation might also inspire us to stay the course through difficult times, but that encouragement to persevere is really an application of the text, not a sound interpretation of it.

2. **What does the interpretation process involve?** To find out what a text means, you need to answer some basic questions. And to do so, you will need some resources besides your Bible. When

you study the Bible, you are studying different cultures and peoples that lived thousands of years ago. Just like my tour group needed guides to help us understand the lands and peoples we visited, so do you. Below I give the central questions you need to ask in the interpretation process. I also tell you the kinds of resources you can consult to find answers to those questions. (For some specific recommendations on resources I've found helpful, see the appendix.)

As you'll see, there's much to consider in the interpretation process. Try not to let it overwhelm or discourage you. When you try interpreting a passage in the next day's exercises, I'll give you some help.

Remember, too, that this is an introduction to the spiritual disciplines. You don't have to master everything, just gain some familiarity with it. You have a lifetime of walking with God to learn and benefit from the disciplines.

So let's get back to the questions you should ask when you seek to interpret the Scriptures.

a. *What is the text's content?* Your discoveries in observation provide the answer to this question. So if you've done your observation homework, you won't have to do it now.

   Your most important resources are a good Bible translation and a Bible dictionary, which is used for looking up information about words, places, people, animals, plants, currency, and the like.

b. *What is the text's context?* Here, too, your observations will provide part of the answer. In observation you looked for context. In interpretation, however, you take the question of context further. The kinds of context you look for are these:

   • **Literary context**. As Howard and William Hendricks explain, "The literary context of any verse is the paragraph of which it is a part, the section of which that paragraph is a part, and the book of which that section is a part. And, given the unity of Scripture, the ultimate context of any book is the entire Bible."[1]

The more you become familiar with the Bible, the easier it will be for you to place a biblical text in its larger literary context, especially in the context of the entire Bible. Meanwhile, however, you can draw on resources such as Bible handbooks, Bible commentaries, Bible dictionaries, and introductions to the Old and New Testaments.

- **Historical context**. The kinds of questions you deal with here are: When did the events described take place? Does this time period have any significance in the wider context of biblical history or teaching? What else was happening in the world at the time that might have some bearing on the interpretation of the text?

  The same resources that you would consult to help you with the literary context will help you with the historical context.

- **Geographical context**. Where did the events described occur? What season was it? What were the terrain and weather like? How far did people have to travel to get there and what would the journey have been like? What was the region known for? Did it boast any cities? If so, how large were they and what were they like?

  Bible atlases and Bible handbooks are your best resources for issues concerning geography.

- **Cultural context**. Here you're interested in discovering as much as you can about the social conditions surrounding and the social influences on the biblical author, his original audience, and the people and events he relates. You want to step into his sandals, see what he saw, hear what he heard, smell the smells, feel the feelings. What was the political situation? How were people treated, especially the weak, the poor, and the vulnerable? Who were treated as outcasts and why? What were the religious institutions and who were their leaders? What kind of commerce was conducted and how was it carried out? What were the prevailing moral and legal codes? How were people educated and how did they spend their spare time? What was a typical family like? How did people get married, and what did couples do who wanted to end their marriages? What language or languages were spoken, and how did they influence the way people thought and behaved? What were the local customs?

It's hard to beat a good Bible commentary when it comes to dealing with questions of cultural context. Other helpful tools are books on the manners and customs of biblical times, books on biblical archaeology, and Bible handbooks.

- **Theological context**. Since the Bible's central focus is God and his dealings with human beings, the theological context of a passage is the most important area of interpretation. In this arena of discovery, you want to find out what the human author believed about God and the created order, especially humankind. You also want to find out what his original audience believed about these matters and how they carried out their religious commitments.

  Other questions you want to explore are: What other portions of Scripture did the author and his audience have available to them at this point in history? What other religions and philosophies were prevalent at the time? Were any of them becoming rivals to or influencing the Jewish or Christian traditions and practices? What was the condition of the relationship between God and his people at the time? Was it a time of blessing? Discipline? Judgment?

Bible commentaries with a theological orientation can be useful here, along with books on biblical, historical, and systematic theology.

c. *What other texts cast light on this text?* Scripture often interprets itself. When it does, it is the most reliable and authoritative commentary on what it means. For instance, after the apostle John records in his Gospel that Peter and the other disciples believed that Jesus was "the Holy One of God," John notes that Jesus said, "'Have I not chosen you, the Twelve? Yet one of you is a devil!'" Following these words, John explains what Jesus meant when he called a disciple a devil: "He meant Judas, the son of Simon Iscariot, who, though one of the Twelve, was later to betray him" (Jn 6:68-71).

In situations such as this, interpreting the Bible is easy. At other times, however, the definitive interpretive key may be several chapters, even books, away. On those occasions, Bibles that contain cross-references will frequently direct you to a few key passages similar or comparable to the one you are studying. However, those references may be inadequate to meet your needs so it is best to have an exhaustive Bible concordance, a commentary or two, and a few theology books at your disposal. They will usually help you locate every Bible reference that could shed even a sliver of light on the text you are studying.

While these questions don't cover everything we could treat under the topic of interpretation, they provide plenty of guidance toward getting a good start. If you need to, reread the material above. In the next day's exercise, you will actually try your hand at interpreting Matthew 6:5-15.

⬇ Going Deeper

Take this book with you to a local Christian bookstore, and see if you can find any of the resources mentioned in the appendix. If the store doesn't have those books, ask the sales clerk to suggest some other books helpful for studying Scripture. Take time to peruse the books available to see what they have to offer you.

Before you go to the bookstore, you might also want to ask your local minister for advice on Bible study tools.

If you don't have a Christian bookstore in your area or you can't get to one, you may know a friend, a church leader, or even another family member who studies the Bible regularly. Ask one of them about the Bible resources he has found useful and see if he will permit you to look through the books he uses in his studies.

Then, if you're able, purchase one or more Bible tools. Begin building your own library of biblical resources. If you can afford even just one Bible reference book per year, you will be investing in a lifetime of potentially renewed

> It cannot be that the people should grow in grace unless they give themselves to reading. A reading people will always be a knowing people. A people who talk much will know little.... Whether you like it or not, read and pray daily. It is for your life; there is no other way; else you will be a trifler all your days.[2]
>
> The Wesleys

understanding and transformed living. I say "potentially" because no study tool can change your life if all it does is collect dust. You must use it in your search for truth, then with truth found, you must make that truth a part of your life. Bible study tools can be a tremendous asset to you in your search for the truth, but they cannot make that truth a vital part of your life—only you can do that.

DAY EIGHT

✍ Getting Started

1. When the disciples asked Jesus to teach them to pray (Luke 11:1), they acknowledged Jesus' ability and authority to teach. As you continue learning the discipline of study, be sure to ask Jesus to teach you through the process. He will always be your best teacher. He uses others to teach you also, especially those who are sensitive to his guidance and immersed in his truth. But because he is alive and active and at work through the Holy Spirit enlightening all those who trust him by faith, he can also teach you directly. So prayerfully ask him to come alongside you in today's lesson.

2. Now turn back to the Lord's Prayer passage (Matthew 6:5-15) you began working on in Week 3, Day 5. Review the text, this time thinking about interpreting it rather than observing it. Pose the questions about interpretation mentioned above, and if at all possible, write your findings next to the observations you made. If there's insufficient room, place your interpretive thoughts on other paper.

   See if the passage and the section it appears in (which is called the Sermon on the Mount and takes up chapters five through seven in Matthew's Gospel) help you interpret Jesus' teaching on prayer. Also check out the material supplied below. It will give you more information to aid you in the interpretation process.

If you do not have a study Bible or Bible study tools, you will be unable to research some issues commonly handled in the interpretation process. That's all right. Working with just your Bible and the following information, you will still learn a great deal about what Jesus wants us to know about prayer.

Major Parallel Passage: Luke 11:1-4.

Meanings of Key Words in Matthew 6:5-15:

Hypocrites (v. 5)—"actors, those who impersonate others."

Reward (v. 5)—"to give back, to repay."

Room (v. 6)—"storeroom, private room, innermost secret room."

Your Father (v. 6)—By attaching the personal pronoun to the Greek word for "father," Jesus is conveying a close parental like relationship with God. As he called God "Abba, Father" (Mk 14:36), so can we who have become God's adopted children through faith in his Son, Jesus Christ (Romans 8:15). *Abba* is the Aramaic word for "father." It expresses a loving, trusting, familial intimacy. Its best English equivalents are "daddy" and "dear father." *Abba* underlies, directly or indirectly, the various Greek versions of Jesus' invocations of God as Father. According to one Bible commentator, "This means that when Jesus gave his disciples the Lord's Prayer, he gave them authority to follow him in addressing God as *'abbā,'* and so gave them a share in his status as Son.... The fact that the church, like Jesus, may say 'Abba' is a fulfillment of God's promise: 'I will be a father to you, and you shall be my sons and daughters' (2 Cor 6:18; a free citation of 2 Sam 7:14...)."[3] For pious Jews, this way of addressing God was unheard of. They did not feel free to address the Lord in such familiar, family terms.

Vain repetitions (v. 7)—"empty words, babbling"; used "either in the sense of repeating the words or babbling or chattering…. Perhaps a reference to the heathen magical formulas, a repetition of meaningless sounds."[4]

Heathen (v. 7)—"Gentiles, pagans, non-Jews."

Hallowed (v. 9)—"to treat as holy, to reverence."

Kingdom (v. 10)—"rule or domain of a king."

This day (v. 11)—"for the coming day."

Daily (v. 11)—"day after day."

Bread (v. 11)—"bread (for the human body)," referring to the necessities, not the luxuries, of life (see Matthew 7:25-34).

Forgive (v. 12)—"to let go, to cancel, to remit, to pardon."

Debts (v. 12)—"what is owed, one's due"; in religious contexts such as this it means "sins" (see Luke 11:4).

Temptation (v. 13)—"temptation, testing."

Deliver (v. 13)—"rescue."

Evil one (v. 13)—"the devil, Satan" (see 1 Peter 5:8-10).

Power (v. 13)—"might, force, strength, ability."

Glory (v. 13)—"honor, fame, praise, repute one has earned and deserves."

Forever (v. 13)—"eternally, without beginning or end."

Amen (v. 13)—"certain, true."

Trespasses (v. 14)—"transgressions, false steps, sins." This word strongly emphasizes the deliberate act of moral wrongdoing along with its fateful consequences.

3. End your time today by thanking the Lord for being your teacher today. Ask him to take what you have learned so far and bring it to mind as you go about each day. Let him begin to show you how his teaching about prayer should affect your life.

Going Deeper

If you have access to a Bible dictionary or Bible encyclopedia, look up the articles on the "Lord's Prayer" and the "Sermon on the Mount." See if they supply some information or interpretive conclusions that shed more light on the meaning of Matthew 6:5-15.

You may find some instances where you have arrived at different conclusions from those taken in the articles. See if you can detect what may have led to the differences. The differences may be due to background information about the text that the authors had and you did not. Or differing views on doctrine may account for the variations in interpretation. It may be the case that the authors caught some details in the text itself that you missed or vice versa. Whatever the reasons for the differences, see if you can figure them out. Doing so will help you better understand why people can read the same text and arrive at different interpretations.

Remain open to revising your conclusions based on the information or insights of other Bible students, especially if they are Christian scholars with a high regard for the integrity and authority of Scripture as God's Word. Learning the Bible is a lifetime process and an investment in personal transformation. We can glean much help along the way if we will pay humble attention to those who have dedicated their lives to studying the Scriptures and passing their findings on to the rest of us.

WEEK 5

An Oasis of Words

It is hard for me to accept that the best I can do is probably not to give but to receive....

... The more I think about the meaning of living and acting in the name of Christ, the more I realize that what I have to offer to others is not my intelligence, skill, power, influence, or connections, but my own human brokenness through which the love of God can manifest itself....

... Every man or woman who lives the Christian life to the full cannot but exercise a deep influence on everyone he or she meets. What continues to fascinate me is that those whose whole mind and heart were directed to God had the greatest impact on other people, while those who tried very hard to be influential were quickly forgotten....

... When I have no eyes for the small signs of God's presence—the smile of a baby, the carefree play of children, the words of encouragement and gestures of love offered by friends—I will always remain tempted to despair.[1]

These personal thoughts about life are excerpted from a journal kept by the Christian minister and teacher Henri Nouwen. The journal covers four months in Nouwen's life, from October 1981 to January 1982. It is, as he puts it, "the personal report of my six-month sojourn in Bolivia and Peru. I wrote it in an attempt to capture the countless impressions, feelings, and ideas that filled my mind and heart day after day. It speaks about new places and people, about new insights and perspectives, and about new joys and anxieties. But the question that runs through all its pages and binds the many varied fragments together is: 'Does God call me to live and work in Latin America in the years to come?'"[2]

In his journal he recounts his experiences in Latin America, and he records his reflections on those experiences, especially in light of his commitment to the Christian faith. Published under the title *¡Gracias!*, Nouwen's entries reveal a man vulnerable before God and his fellow human beings. They show us a man growing deeper in his understanding of and appreciation for the Creator and Savior. They allow us to enter the warp and woof of one man's life during his time of searching for God's will. *¡Gracias!* is an oasis of words flowing from the Fountain of life (John 4:13-14; 6:35; 7:37-39) and God's work in Nouwen's life.

This is what the spiritual discipline of journaling can bring to a human being. It opens doors to one's mind and heart, as it encourages and accomplishes an ever-engaging conversation between a creature and the Creator. That's right. God still speaks. And those who have the willingness to listen will hear his voice. Journaling is a form of listening. It is also a vehicle for talking. It is, in short, a tool for conversing with the Lord. As Rev. Gordon MacDonald says, "The main value of a journal is as a tool for listening to the quiet Voice that comes out of the garden of the private world. Journal-keeping serves as a wonderful tool for withdrawing and communing with the Father."[3]

For the next two weeks, we will concentrate on the discipline of journaling. This week, our focus will be on what journaling involves and how to get started doing it.

DAY NINE

✎ Getting Started

A spiritual journal can contain all kinds of entries, such as:

- records of daily or memorable events;
- thoughts;
- feelings;
- questions and doubts;
- beliefs;
- impressions, including what one senses God is saying;
- prayer requests and answers;
- Bible verses;
- meditations on Scripture;
- studies of Scripture;
- notable quotes;
- prayers;
- confessions;
- misgivings;
- thanksgivings;
- dreams and ambitions;
- concerns and anxieties.

The entries can be long or short, in longhand or shorthand, printed or in cursive, typed or inputted. And they can be made daily, weekly, or irregularly.

In other words, there are really few requirements in journal-keeping. As I see it, there are four: (1) you must be honest and vulnerable; (2) you must be ready to listen as well as to speak; (3) you

> The keeping of a pilgrim journal requires a conscious, unswerving commitment to honesty with one's self… the first requirement for growth in self-understanding…. This takes a lot of courage, a lot of endurance, a commitment to press on when we want to shrink back..[4]
>
> Elizabeth O'Connor

must be willing to be humbled; and (4) you must be willing to change. I'm tempted to add making regular journal entries to the list, but that is not essential, though desirable.

With these thoughts in mind, let's get started on the journey of journal-keeping.

The first thing you need for journaling is a journal. It can be a spiral notebook, a binder with notebook paper, a bound book with blank or lined pages, or anything else you feel comfortable writing in. You may already have a journal and have some entries in it already. However, if you don't already have something you can use for your journal-keeping, take this opportunity to fill the need.

From here on, I will be asking you to complete many exercises in your journal. If you don't have one, you won't have the space in the rest of this book to make numerous requested entries. So don't put this off. *Get a journal today.* Once you have one, move ahead with the next day's exercises.

D A Y   T E N

✑ Getting Started

1. Now that you have a journal, give some thought to how you want to set it up. For instance, my life is complicated enough without making my journal-keeping a complex science. So what I use is a bound book that contains blank pages. When I make a journal entry, I begin by writing down the month, day, and year, then I place under that heading my thoughts, feelings, recollections, prayers… whatever I wish to put down on paper for that day.

   This method gives me a good deal of flexibility. One day's entry may be no more than a sentence, while another day's may go on for several pages. The length doesn't matter because I have not imposed a structure on my journal that carries any preset limits. I write until my time runs out or my words do. Then when I decide to make another entry, I simply add the appropriate calendar information as my heading and begin writing again. Straightforward and simple.

Other people like to divide their journal into sections. One section might be for written prayers, another for recording favorite quotes or Bible verses, another for listing prayer requests and answers, and another for writing down the day's events, impressions, feelings, and the like.

You may have a different approach in mind, or you might even want to experiment with various set ups. That's fine. Just take some time now to decide what approach you want to try first, then arrange your journal accordingly.

By the way, remember who your best Teacher is. Bring him into this process through prayer. He may not give you word-for-word, step-by-step direction, but he will participate in some way.

2. In your journal, make an entry dedicating your journal-keeping to the Lord. You may even want to put it in the form of a prayer.

When I began journaling many years ago, I wanted my mind and heart focused on God from the very start. I also wanted my journaling to be an offering to him. So this is what I wrote:

Father—

I dedicate this journal to you, Lord, the Creator of language, the eternal Reason and Word. I want to know you, to enter into fellowship with you while I'm on earth in preparation for the intimacy I will enjoy with you in heaven. Please use my thoughts, words, and feelings to draw me closer to you, to increase my finite understanding of your infinite essence and mysterious ways.

Only in knowing you will I come to know myself and to understand others. So I turn to you, the beginning and end of my search.

What you say or how you say it is not sacrosanct. What matters is that your words come from your heart, that they are genuine. Just speak to the One who loves you unconditionally. Pour out your heart's desires. He will hear you and respond.

WEEK 6

Lifetime Benefits

Like the other spiritual disciplines, journaling has many benefits. A journal provides an outlet for expressing thoughts and feelings you may not be ready to share with others at this time in your life. In it you can detail your self-doubts or struggles with family members or friends. You can verbalize your dissatisfactions with your marriage, children, or career. You can work through painful experiences or come to terms with lost opportunities and broken dreams. You can pour out your hurt, confusion, and frustrations in imaginary letters to people that you will never mail. In the process, you bring to light and objectify what would otherwise remain hidden and subjective. This is frequently an eye-opening experience that can bring clarity and healing in your life.

Accomplished Christian author Madeleine L'Engle knows this to be true. In her book *Walking on Water*, she talks about her journaling experience as her "free psychiatrist's couch." "If I can write things out I can see them," she writes. "They are not trapped within my own subjectivity." She provides an example of how journaling helped her see through the pain of a situation and find resolution:

Not long ago someone I love said something which wounded me grievously, and I was desolate that this person could possibly have made such a comment to me.

So, in great pain, I crawled to my journal and wrote it all out in a great burst of self-pity. And when I had set it down, when I had it before me, I saw that something I myself had said had called forth the words which had hurt me so. It had, in fact, been my own fault. But I would never have seen it if I had not written it out.[1]

A journal is also a place where you can brainstorm without fearing ridicule. Here you can articulate ideas, plan new inventions, or propose possible solutions to problems. As a writer with a wide variety of interests, I frequently use my journal to record my musings about book or article ideas. I will outline project ideas, sort through any hesitations about pursuing them, and record stories I may want to use or feelings I may want to recall. Many of my ideas will never go beyond my journal, but most of the ones that find publishing homes were born first in my journal.

Journaling can also give you space to blow off steam safely. We all get angry and hurt, and at times all of us want to strike out at someone, even if only verbally. A journal can be a place where we can do that without inflicting any emotional or physical damage to another person. Some of the psalmists used the written word to express their intense feelings about people they despised or hated. Here are some choice selections from Psalm 109, which David wrote and whom God described as "a man after my own heart" (Acts 13:22; see also 1 Samuel 13:14):

> Appoint an evil man to oppose him;...
> When he is tried, let him be found guilty,
>   and may his prayers condemn him.
> May his days be few;
>   may another take his place of leadership.
> May his children be fatherless
>   and his wife a widow.
> May his children be wandering beggars;
>   may they be driven from their ruined homes.
> May a creditor seize all he has;
>   may strangers plunder the fruits of his labor.
> May no one extend kindness to him
>   or take pity on his fatherless children....
> May their sins always remain before the Lord,
>   that he may cut off the memory of them from the earth....
> May this be the Lord's payment to my accusers,
>   to those who speak evil of me.   Psalms 109:6-12, 15, 20

The eventual goal of such outbursts is to bring them under the scrutiny of God and allow him to help us resolve them in obedience to his will. His desire is that we love even our enemies and do all we can to be at peace with all people (Luke 6:27-36; Romans 12:18). This is hard work. In fact, it's impossible for us to do apart from the Holy Spirit's ministry in our lives (Galatians 5:16-26). Nevertheless, essential to the process of bringing our anger and hatred under control is giving them a safe place to vent. Our journals can serve that need.

Another benefit journal-keeping provides is a chronicle of our journey with God. Human beings are forgetful creatures. We have trouble remembering things when times are good and easy. But add stress, pain, or upheaval to the scenario, and our ability to recollect crashes like a computer's hard drive. God knows this about us. It's one reason he has given us a written revelation. In the Bible he inspired its human authors to repeat certain events and their significance, sometimes scores of times. You can't complete reading the Old Testament without hearing over and over again about the Creation, the Abrahamic promise, the Exodus, the Mosaic Law, and Israel's complaining and idolatry. You can't get through the New Testament without reading reference after reference to Jesus Christ and the fullness of salvation available through him. God even gave us four biographical perspectives on Jesus' life (the four Gospels), making it impossible for us to see the New Testament as anything less than a witness to the incarnation of God's own Son in history for humankind's redemption.

Some of the Bible's most significant words are "remember" and "do not forget" (Deuteronomy 8:11-20; 1 Chronicles 16:12-13; John 15:20-21; Ephesians 2:11-13; James 1:25). Even the rituals recall the events that gave the church life and make it possible for it to be an ongoing conduit of life to others (e.g., see Matthew 28:19 and Romans 6:3-4 on baptism; Matthew 26:26-28 and 1 Corinthians 11:23-26 on the Lord's Supper or Eucharist).

> To satisfy my curiosity, I decided to experiment, and began keeping [a journal] for myself.
>
> At first it was difficult. I felt self-conscious. . . . But slowly the self-consciousness began to fade, and I found myself sharing in the journal more and more of the thoughts that flooded my inner spirit. . . .
>
> Slowly I began to realize that the journal was helping me come to grips with an enormous part of my inner person that I had never been fully honest about. No longer could fears and struggles remain inside without definition. They were surfaced and confronted. And I became aware, little by little, that God's Holy Spirit was directing many of the thoughts and insights as I wrote. On paper, the Lord and I were carrying on a personal communion.[2]
>
> Gordon MacDonald

Through journaling you can record your witness of God's work in your life and the lives of those around you. By creating a written account, you make it easier to remember. If you ever forget, you can then turn to your journal and rediscover what the Lord has done.

One last benefit I would like to mention is self-discovery. The Bible calls on each of us to examine ourselves and our work so we might arrive at an accurate understanding of who we are, what we have accomplished, and whether we are standing in the faith (Romans 12:3, 16; 2 Corinthians 13:5; Galatians 6:3-4). A journal can be a place where you take what is inside you and bring it into the open. There you can explore it and seek to keep what is good and purge what is evil.

I warn you, though, the work of self-discovery will be messy and disturbing at times. You may find haunting memories you had long suppressed. There may surface renewed feelings of resentment you thought were history. You might glory in a job done well, while finally facing the reality of relationships damaged or health sacrificed in the process. Don't let such prospects deter you from doing the spiritual spade work. God wants you to become all he has created you to be. If you are in Christ, you can be encouraged by the fact that the Spirit is already at work in you, striving to bring to completion the "good work" already begun in you (Philippians 1:6; see also 1 Corinthians 1:8; Ephesians 5:25-27; Colossians 1:21-23; 1 Thessalonians 3:12-13). But good cannot coexist with bad. God loves us enough to want to see us fully good, completely whole. Achieving that end will be painful and humbling, but whatever we suffer getting there will be trifling compared with all we will gain (Romans 8:18-23; 2 Corinthians 4:16-18).

Contrary to the claims of some people, God's perfecting work in us is work in which we are expected and encouraged to participate. "As obedient children," the apostle Peter writes, "do not conform to the evil desires you had when you lived in ignorance. But just as he who called you is holy, so be holy in all you do" (1 Pt 1:14-15). The great missionary Paul concurs: "Count yourselves dead to sin but alive to God in Christ Jesus. Therefore do not let sin reign in your mortal body so that you obey its evil desires. Do not offer the parts of your body to sin, as instruments of wickedness, but rather offer yourselves to God, as those who have been brought from death to life; and offer the parts of your body to him as instruments of righteousness. For sin shall not be your master, because you are not under law, but under grace" (Rom 6:11-14). The Christian life is not summed up in the oft-repeated motto, "Let go, let God." We are not passive bystanders but active participants. Our call is, "Let us go with God." He leads; we follow. He commands; we obey. He convicts; we confess. He forgives; we accept and praise. He sanctifies; we pursue sanctified living.

Our everything is raised to new heights and transformed in

him who makes all things new. In Christ, he makes us new creatures (2 Corinthians 5:17); gives us new names (Revelation
2:17); calls us to serve under a new covenant with new commands (Hebrews 9:15; 10:19-25; John 13:34); and exhorts us to
live in light of the coming new heaven and new earth (2 Peter
3:10-13). "I am making everything new!" the ascended Jesus
exclaims (Rv 21:5). And he does so, at least in part, by graciously
and lovingly enabling our feeble efforts and making them a part
of his unfailing, perfecting work. In this he crowns us with glory.
He brings us alongside himself and allows us to become coworkers with him (John 14:12; 15:4-5; 1 Corinthians 3:6-9; 2
Corinthians 6:1; Colossians 1:9-12, 24-29; 4:11-12).

Part of that new creation work is re-creating you and me.
When we practice the spiritual discipline of journaling, we help
further the work of restoration within us. So let's return to the
task he has given us.

DAY ELEVEN
✍ Getting Started

1. Over the last few weeks you have observed and interpreted
   Matthew 6:5-15. Now it's time to apply it to your life. Your
   journal-keeping time provides an excellent opportunity to think
   through and record applications. Before you do, I would like to
   introduce you to the application step of the Bible study process.

   Biblical application can cover anything from the most personal, intimate issues of a person's life to matters of broader
   ecclesiastical or social concern. In some scriptural passages, the
   application will be clear and straightforward. In others you will
   need to ponder the text's meaning for a while before any
   application ideas come to mind. The Matthew 6 passage
   should be uncomplicated.

No matter what Bible text is your focus, there are several questions you can pose that will help you surface applications for your life.[3]

- *Is there an example to follow?* There are many people in Scripture worthy of emulation. Perhaps you can learn from the way they face temptations and testings, or stand up to demanding people, or articulate their faith, or offer praise to God, or provide leadership in difficult straits, or parent their children, or love their spouse.

- *Is there an example to avoid?* Not all examples are worth repeating or modeling your life after. The Bible tells about believers and unbelievers making mistakes, some serious, even fatal. By learning from their mistakes, you can avoid a lot of pain.

- *Is there a sin to confess?* Better than any other book in the world, the Bible reveals our sin. "For the word of God is living and active. Sharper than any double-edged sword, it penetrates even to dividing soul and spirit, joints and marrow; it judges the thoughts and attitudes of the heart" (Heb 4:12). When we're struck to the bone, we should fall to our knees and turn our eyes toward heaven in repentance, remembering that God is quick to forgive those who humbly seek his mercy and grace.

- *Is there a promise to trust?* The Bible is full of promises God has made. Some were only for certain individuals, while others were just for certain groups or nations. Many promises, however, are timeless. John 3:16 is one of these: "For God so loved the world that he gave his one and only Son, that whoever believes in him shall not perish but have eternal life." When you find such promises in Scripture, embrace them. God always honors his promises (Titus 1:1-3; Hebrews 10:23).

- *Is there a prayer to repeat or model?* The Bible is a treasure chest of prayers. It contains prayers of praise and confession, petition and thanksgiving, confidence and confusion, joy and depression, anger and reconciliation, anxiety and trust. You can learn much from the prayers of others. Many prayers in Scripture can be spoken as your own.

- *Is there a command to obey?* Jesus made it quite clear that loving him means obeying him (John 14:15). And the apostle John intertwined love and obedience when he stated, "This is love for God: to obey his commands. And his commands are not burdensome" (1 Jn 5:3). If you ever wonder what God's will is for your life, consider his commands. They will give you plenty of guidance.

- *Is there a condition to meet?* Many of God's promises depend on our doing something first. For example, when Jesus says, "Come to me, all you who are weary and burdened, and I will give you rest" (Mt 11:28), the condition to meet is wrapped up in the call "Come to me." If we don't turn to him, we will not find the rest only he can give. God always delivers on his promises, but sometimes we have to act before he will.

- *Is there a doctrine to accept and understand?* Doctrinal riches abound in Scripture. Teachings about God, nature, people, angels, demons, morality, relationships, salvation, the church, heaven, hell, and many more subjects are numerous and frequently quite detailed. But the Bible is not a systematic presentation of theology. Rather, within the context of God's work in human history, doctrine slowly unfolds. So, to learn all the Bible has to say about a particular subject, you will have a good deal of biblical ground to cover. You won't be able to go to just one chapter or one book to find all the pertinent information. On the other hand, what you will unearth in just one book of Scripture will usually give you plenty to adopt and contemplate.

- *Is there a heresy to reject?* Not all beliefs are true. The Bible talks about people who believe in false gods or pursue dead-end paths to salvation. It tells about earthly rulers who command their subjects to worship them as deity. It shows people following false messiahs, believing that the stars and planets determine their destiny, and accepting the lie that hoarding wealth will bring them happiness. It warns us about false teachers and others who distort the truth about Jesus Christ and his gospel message. Jesus said the truth would make us free (Jn 8:32). If the truth liberates, error enslaves. When the Scriptures expose heresies, you should take note so you can avoid falling prey to them.

- *Is there a social challenge to face?* The Bible calls on us to clothe the naked, feed the hungry, defend the defenseless, right wrongs, and engage in other challenging activities in our society (Matthew 25:34-40; James 1:27; 2:15-16). When a passage speaks to social concerns, you should consider how God may want to draw upon your talents, gifts, and other resources to help meet one or more of those needs.

- *Is there a personal difficulty to confront?* Studying Scripture may unearth deep-seated hurts that never healed. It may put you face to face with a character flaw you have tried to ignore or rationalize. It may even uncover poor attitudes or bad habits. Whatever personal issue it touches and no matter how deeply its touch penetrates, accept the pain as the work of a caring surgeon. The Bible's work may feel like a sword thrust at times, but its design is to cut out only that which is harmful to us. So bear the wounds and stay on the operating table until the heavenly Surgeon has completed his work. Follow his advice in his Word. You will be a healthier person for it.

- *Is there a relationship to improve?* Marriage, parenting, friendship, employer-employee relationships, citizenship, church ministry... the Bible covers these relationships and more. It tells us the pitfalls to avoid, the habits to cultivate, the characteristics to look for, the values to prize, and the ways to heal fractures. There is no better self-help book on how to improve your relationships than the Bible.

- *Is there a reason to offer thanks to God?* At the heart of all that the Bible teaches is the attitude of gratitude to God. Its absence leads to corruption and idolatry (Romans 1:21-32). Its cultivation brings God's peace and blessing; it places us in his revealed will; and it paves the way for our enjoyment of his creation (Philippians 4:6-7; 1 Thessalonians 5:18; 1 Timothy 4:1-5). God has given us so much for which to be grateful. If he never did anything more, he deserves our thanks.

- *Are there some questions to pursue?* Sometimes your interpretation of a biblical passage will raise questions, even troubling ones. God's dealings may appear harsh or unfair or too lenient. You may be disturbed reading about a prophet who carries out God's bidding and suffers for it. Perhaps you will come across two accounts of the same event that seem to differ. Or maybe you will study a text that teaches or describes something that strikes you as preposterous or incredulous. Whenever such questions arise, you should write them down and commit yourself to seeking answers to them. Over my two decades of studying the Scriptures, I have raised hundreds of such questions and I have found good answers to most of them. In many cases other Bible texts have supplied the missing pieces. Frequently, however, I have found invaluable help in secondary sources, such as Bible commentaries, dictionaries, lexical aids, and theology books. Never suppress or ignore your questions. Only by asking them and looking for answers to them will you ever resolve them.

2. Now refer to your interpretation notes of Matthew 6:5-15. In light of the application questions listed above and your life situation, consider how you would apply the teaching of this biblical text. Record your conclusions in your journal.

Take your time. You will have the opportunity during part of the next day's exercises to finish this task.

Remember to ask the Teacher *par excellence* to guide you through today's exercises. You want him to point out areas of your life to which Matthew 6 pertains. He will, too. Of that you can be sure.

Going Deeper

After I have spent time studying and applying Scripture, I like to get away to mull over what I've learned or zero in on some truth that really struck home. Consider trying this, too. Take off to your own getaway place. Perhaps it's a park or a zoo. Maybe it's a nearby field or lake. It could even be your own backyard, patio, balcony, or study. Some people even like coffee houses or restaurants. Think of somewhere to go, and take your journal with you.

Once you're there, linger over what you've studied in Matthew. If there are one or two discoveries you found particularly poignant, fascinating, or perhaps troubling, focus your mind on those. Think about them, especially in light of your own beliefs, habits, relationships, and any other pertinent aspects of your life. Use your journal to write out the findings of your probes.

Also, listen to the Holy Spirit. He will speak to you through your thoughts and emotions. He may even use your surroundings to help enlighten you about some truth or impress you with a truth you may be struggling to accept.

Record in your journal all that comes to you.

When you're done, review your journal entry. Then, in your journal, express thanksgiving to the Lord for being with you during this time, and ask him to help you discern over the coming weeks that which is true and that which is not. The truths are ultimately from him. The rest is not.

As you mature in the Christian faith, your discernment abilities will increase accordingly, which only makes sense. The more we understand God and walk in the steps he wants us to, the better we will be able to pick out his voice from all the other voices clamoring for our attention.

DAY TWELVE

✍️ Getting Started

1. For the last time, return to Matthew 6:5-15 and write in your journal any other applications you find. And once again pray for the Lord's guidance before you begin.

2. In all likelihood, you have come up with more applications than you can successfully make a part of your life in the next few weeks, perhaps even months. There are several ways you can handle this problem.

One way is to choose one or two of your application conclusions and make those your focus until they become second nature to you. Then go back and choose another application point or two and work on those until they, too, become routine. Like the Duracell rabbit, you just keep going and going and going until you run out of applications to make. I have often used this approach to great benefit over the years. It keeps the applications to a manageable number, and it allows me the time I need to incorporate them into my experience.

Another helpful option is to select no more than a few of your application decisions and work on them simultaneously. When they become habits, select a few more and do the same until you have exhausted your application list. This approach has also worked well for me, as long as I have not tried to accomplish more than I could handle. At times I have had to cut back my list, bringing me closer in approach to the first option I mentioned.

Sometimes, no matter how many applications I pull out of a text, one stands out above the rest. It strikes me in a way the others don't. I just know that if I do not accomplish anything else the passage teaches, I must work on this one application. I take it and concentrate on it to the exclusion of all others. I may not return to the rest of my application list for months or even years. However, I will give my attention to that one application decision until I am confident I own it.

Whatever approach you choose, make sure you do at least two things: (1) Keep your plan flexible, realizing your individuality and changing life situation may require you to make some adjustments along the way; and (2) continually and prayerfully rely on God to guide you in your application decisions and to enable you to take the steps necessary to bring them to fruition. Keep in mind what Jesus said: "I am the vine; you are the branches. If a man remains in me and I in him, he will bear much fruit; apart from me you can do nothing" (Jn 15:5). Branches wither and die when separated from the vine (v. 6). As long as we stay connected to Christ, which prayer (and the other disciplines) help us do, we will bear fruit in our lives. That's a promise from the Son of God to us.

Now take the time you have left to select which application decisions you will work on and how you plan to weave them into the fabric of your life. In your journal, record your plan of action, then begin carrying it out. Remember to include God in the entire process, from selection to formulation to execution. He knows you better than anyone, including yourself. So he knows best what you need to change and how that change should take place. Ask him to guide your steps and redirect your path if necessary. That's a prayer request he will always honor when the petitioner asks with a sincere heart.

Going Deeper

To me, one of the most interesting aspects of the Lord's Prayer is its community orientation. The one who prays it is not told to pray in the first person singular but in the first person plural. Jesus says, "Our Father," not "My Father"; "Give us," not "Give me"; "Forgive us," not "Forgive me." It would not be wrong for us to pray it in the first person singular. Obviously, if I am a member of the Christian community by faith in Christ, then the Lord's Prayer is applicable to me. On the other hand, Jesus' use of the first person plural indicates that his prayer is first and foremost communal. It is a prayer for the believing community to pray together and for its members. It is meant to sensitize us to the spiritual and material needs of other Christians. In fact, just before Jesus teaches on prayer in the Sermon on the Mount, he talks about how we should give to the needy (Matthew 6:1-4). While he has more than just the Christian needy in mind, he certainly does not mean less. Christians should pray for one another and take care of one another. (We'll deal with this facet of the Christian life more fully as we work through the other spiritual disciplines, particularly the discipline of service.)

Take some time to pray for your church's leaders and members, using the Lord's Prayer as your guide. If you're aware of any specific needs, intercede for those especially. Ask the Lord to help you consider how you might be part of his answer in meeting any of those needs. Then do as he directs, using Matthew 6:1-4 as your guiding counsel on giving.

✓ Checking In

This ends your first six weeks worth of exercises practicing the spiritual disciplines. I hope you are beginning to see some changes occur in your life. They may be small, which is fine. Most changes start that way. If they are firmly planted in good soil and nurtured properly, they will grow over time into large, beautiful trees with deep roots and healthy, spreading limbs that invite people to sit under them and there find cover from the vicissitudes of life.

Whether you see any significant changes occurring yet or not, I urge you to keep going. When you're in training and running the race of the Christian life, you may grow tired or discouraged and want to quit. You're not alone. I have felt that way at times, and so have many believers who have gone before you. Did you know that even Jesus wanted to quit at one point in his life?

The night before Jesus was arrested on trumped-up charges, he took his disciples to the Mount of Olives and walked a short distance away from them to pray. There he asked his Father to spare him from the humiliation and excruciating death he knew awaited him. In agony he called out to the Father. Three times he made the same petition: "Father, if you are willing, take this cup from me; yet not my will, but yours be done" (Lk 22:42; cf. Mt

26:36-43). He prayed so hard that he broke out into a sweat that was "like drops of blood falling to the ground" (Lk 22:44). Jesus felt overwhelmed. He wanted out. He did not want to go to the cross. And yet, as terrified and desperate as he was, he managed to maintain, however weakly, his submission to the Father's will. "Yet not my will, but yours be done."

The Father, though, did not let Jesus off the hook. He allowed Jesus' persecutors to nail him to a cross and let him hang there until he died. Jesus knew that was the plan and that to fulfill the Scriptures he had to suffer and die (Luke 9:22; 12:50; 18:31-32). So he went. Reluctantly. Hoping for a way of escape. Still, he obeyed. He ran his race and completed it victoriously.

What did the Father do in return? He raised his Son from the dead and carried him into heaven and gave him authority over all things (Ephesians 1:20-23; 1 Peter 3:21-22).

Reflecting on these events, the writer of the letter to the Hebrews exhorted his readers to look to Jesus when they became discouraged and wanted to give up: "Let us throw off everything that hinders and the sin that so easily entangles, and let us run with perseverance the race marked out for us. Let us fix our eyes on Jesus, the author and perfecter of our faith, who for the joy set before him endured the cross, scorning its shame, and sat down at the right hand of the throne of God. Consider him who endured such opposition from sinful men, so that you will not grow weary and lose heart" (Heb 12:1-3).

This Jesus is our example. He is also our Savior, Lord, and strength. Nothing can defeat him. How could it? He holds the reins of authority over everything. "If God is for us, who can be against us?" asks Paul rhetorically (Rom 8:31). As long as we stay focused on Jesus and abide in him, we cannot ultimately fail. Through him we can always find the resources we need to overcome whatever obstacles cross our paths, whether those hurdles come from inside or outside us.

So I encourage you to press on in him. He will abundantly reward your efforts even as he enables you to carry on.

WEEK 7

Food for the Soul

Food and Fellowship Time Change

Please take note that the fellowship time for Sunday afternoon has been changed from 5:00 to 4:00. We moved it back an hour so everyone would have more time to enjoy each other and the Lord before the 6:00 service. Remember, if your last name begins with any letter between A and J, bring a main dish; with any letter between K and P, bring a side dish; and with any letter between Q and Z, bring a dessert. Drinks will be provided. There will be plenty of food and fun for all, so come join us for some fellowship together in the Lord.

This notice could appear in just about any church in our culture. I've seen many like it over the years. It reveals a fact about Christian gatherings rarely thought about, much less scrutinized. This fact is that in Christian circles food is almost always equated with fellowship. I can't remember the last time I saw a church or Christian group advertise a fellowship time without highlighting food. Food and fellowship are like Siamese twins—inseparable.

Surely one reason this is so is because it's virtually impossible to get Christians to do much of anything without having something tasty available to devour. Donuts or bagels with fresh brewed coffee are a good lure to get believers out of bed for an early morning prayer meeting or Bible study. Potlucks with homemade desserts do the trick when pastors want to fill those Sunday late morning or evening worship services. The promise of pizza or sub sandwiches can tempt even the busiest Christians to come out to the church and do yardwork or cleanup. Promise them food and they will come. Without food, get-togethers and ministry come to a halt.

As important as food has become, I'm surprised churches don't have a salaried pastoral position to make certain the food chain experiences no breaks. I can just see the ad for such a post:

> *Wanted:* A connoisseur of fellowship cuisine to become our Minister of Nourishment. This person will strive to ensure continued growth at First Church of the Unending Feast. Must have at least five years of proven cooking experience and three years service as a successful caterer. A master of divinity degree and agreement with our church doctrinal statement are preferred but not mandatory. Please bring your résumé and references, copies of your ten best recipes, and samples of your cooking talents to the Tasting Committee at First Church of the Unending Feast, 8882 Much Boulevard, in Gullet's Gorge.

There's nothing wrong with satisfying bodily palates while guiding people to spiritual food. After all, we are embodied souls. On the other hand, many Christians have forgotten—perhaps never realized—the fact that temporarily depriving the body of its cravings can create healthier souls and bodies. Overly nourished bodies can be a sign of undernourished souls.

Earthly food often controls our lives more than heavenly food. "Follow your nose, it always knows," asserts the colorful Toucan Sam for his cold cereal of choice. "Obey your thirst," the soft drink ad says in a demanding tone. Eat this and drink that so you will become attractive, famous, healthy, or acceptable to the right people. So we stuff our mouths and drown our thirst, but the promised benefits don't follow. Instead, our cupboards and bodies overflow, and our medical and clothing bills increase. We need a change in diet. Our menus should reflect all that we are. We need food for our souls as well as for our bodies. What's the solution? The spiritual discipline of fasting.

> Fasting confirms our utter dependence upon God by finding in him a source of sustenance beyond food. Through it, we learn by experience that God's Word to us is a life substance, that it is not food... alone that gives life, but also the words that proceed from the mouth of God (Mt 4:4).[1]
>
> Dallas Willard

This spiritual discipline normally involves abstaining from bodily nourishment for spiritual purposes. Fasting can convey a contrite spirit over our sin. It can help us concentrate on heavenly matters rather than on simply earthly ones. It can give us more time to devote ourselves to prayer or to another spiritual endeavor because we are not spending the time preparing a meal, eating one, or cleaning up after one. It can be used as a sacrifice of thanksgiving or as a cry for God's protection and deliverance. Whatever the purpose, fasting is not a means to get God's attention or force him to bow to our wishes. Fasting is for *our* benefit. It attunes us to him and his will, and it surfaces issues within us that either facilitate or hinder God's transforming work in our lives and the lives of those we touch.

The Bible is filled with examples of individual and corporate fasts. In the Old Testament some persons who fasted were Moses (Deuteronomy 9:9), Israel's King David (2 Samuel 12:15-23), the prophet Elijah (1 Kings 19:8), the seer Daniel (Daniel 10:3), and Queen Esther (Esther 4:16). In the New Testament the prophetess Anna (Luke 2:37), John the Baptist's disciples (Mark 2:18), the apostle Paul (2 Corinthians 11:27), and the God-man Jesus Christ (Matthew 4:2) all fasted. Along with individuals, groups of people also fasted: the nations of Israel and Judah (Judges 20:26; 2 Chronicles 20:1-4), some warriors under Israel's King Saul (1 Samuel 31:11-13), the Ninevites (Jonah 3:5-8), the Hebrew exiles before and after returning to Jerusalem (Ezra 8:21-23; Nehemiah 9:1), and the congregation of the Antiochene church (Acts 13:1-3) are just a few of the many examples recorded in Scripture.

After biblical times, the discipline of fasting continued. Church history records numerous examples of believers who abstained from food in their pursuit of God. Some more well-known figures are Tertullian, Augustine, Anselm, Aquinas, Teresa of Ávila, Francis of Assisi, Clare (founder of the Poor Clares), Martin Luther, John Calvin, David Brainerd, John Wesley, John Knox, Jonathan Edwards, and Charles Finney. The *Didache*, a first-century book of Christian instruction, calls on believers to fast weekly on Wednesdays and Fridays. And in many church traditions, times of fasting often precede liturgical events (such as communion, baptism, and ordination); seasons (especially Easter, Christmas, and Pentecost); and certain saints' days.

Fasting is undoubtedly a fixed and important part of the spiritual development of believers. God's people have recognized it as such for thousands of years. So let's begin to discover what so many others have. Let's turn our attention to appreciating and practicing this discipline of the Christian life.

SPECIAL NOTE

FOR MEDICAL REASONS, some people should not fast at all or should limit their fasts to partial ones. People who are undernourished or suffer from nervous exhaustion fall in this category, as do pregnant women and diabetics.

If you have any doubts about your body's ability to handle a time of fasting, seek out the advice of your doctor first.

If anything more than a partial fast is unadvisable at this time, limit yourself to that whenever you're directed in this book to engage in the discipline of fasting.

If you are advised to abstain from all forms of food fasting, then substitute the lifestyle (non-food)-fasting exercises for the food-fasting exercises. Whether you end up food fasting or lifestyle fasting, still complete the study sections that follow. Although they are directly concerned with food fasts, they reveal principles that can be applied to lifestyle fasts as well.

DAY THIRTEEN

✍ Getting Started

The Christian practice of fasting is grounded in what Jesus taught on the subject. Interestingly enough, much of his teaching on fasting occurs immediately after his teaching on prayer, both of which occur in his Sermon on the Mount. This section of Scripture will be our focus today.

1. Turn to Matthew 6:16-18 and read it a few times. You might try reading it aloud once or twice as well.

2. Spend some time observing the details of the text and interpreting its message. You already completed much of your contextual work when you studied the Lord's Prayer, so your study of this passage should not take nearly as long. Write your observations and interpretations in your journal.

3. Now, in light of your study of Jesus' teaching, complete the following statements using your own words:

When I fast, I should not _____

_____

_____ .

When fast, I should _____

_____

_____ .

When I fast as I should, I can expect _____

_____

_____ .

Food-Fasting Exercise

4. With this divine direction in mind, begin your practice of fasting with a *partial* fast. A partial fast is where you limit your diet without abstaining from all foods. Choose a food or family of foods you normally eat each day. Then go through an entire day this week where you don't eat that food and don't substitute another food for it. You may feel a craving for the absent food. If so, ask the Lord to help you overcome the urge to break your fast.

When you pass up eating the food you would normally, use it as an opportunity to thank the Lord for all his provisions and perhaps to take something before him that is pressing on you or someone you know.

Lifestyle-Fasting Exercise

5. If for health reasons you should not engage in a food fast right now, consider abstaining from something else. For example, a partial *lifestyle* fast for you might be refusing to make or answer telephone calls, watch television, or read the newspaper. You could refrain from listening to the radio or stereo. You could forego talking, sleeping, gardening, or driving. Whatever you choose, it should be an activity you normally do and one you can sacrifice for at least three consecutive hours on a single day.

Going Deeper

Choose one other day this week to practice a partial fast, whether it concerns food or lifestyle activities, so you engage in the discipline on two days rather than just one.

Also, if you have the tools and interest, look up fasting in a Bible dictionary or Bible encyclopedia to gain a more detailed portrait of fasting in biblical times.

Checking In

I did not mention anything about praying at the beginning of today's exercise. Hopefully by now you don't need me to mention it. The discipline of prayer should be becoming more habitual now. If not, take this as a gentle reminder that each day's worth of exercises should be bathed in prayer.

As you have prayed, have you noticed God helping you comprehend the material and apply it to your life? If someone asked you, "How do you know God is answering your prayers for assistance?" what would you tell them?

Don't be discouraged if you are still unaware of God's activity in the learning process. It takes time to recognize the signs. As we go along, you will learn more that will help you see God at work more easily.

DAY FOURTEEN

✍ Getting Started

When Jesus taught about fasting in the Sermon on the Mount, he said "*When* you fast" (Mt 6:16), not "if" or "whether." He introduced the disciplines of giving and praying in the same way: "*when* you give to the needy" (v. 2) and "*when* you pray" (v. 5). Just as he expected his followers to pray and give, so he expected them to fast.

However, while Jesus was on earth carrying out his ministry in Palestine, he did not require his disciples to fast. This bothered the disciples of John the Baptist, who apparently fasted regularly. So they asked Jesus about this discrepancy. He answered them with an analogy. He compared being present with his disciples with a bridegroom being present with his guests. Just as the guests of a bridegroom feast in celebration while the groom is with them, so the disciples of Jesus celebrate their Master's presence while he is with them. On the other hand, Jesus added, "The time will come when the bridegroom will be taken from them; then they will fast" (Mt 9:15). That time is now, the church age.

Before his crucifixion, resurrection, and ascension into heaven, Jesus told the twelve disciples that in his absence he would send the Holy Spirit. The Spirit would come from the Father in the Son's name. He would teach the disciples "all things" and bring Jesus' teachings to their remembrance (John 14:26). The Spirit would also testify about Jesus (15:26) and "convict the world of guilt in regard to sin and right-eousness and judgment" (16:8). When the Spirit came in power on the Day of Pentecost, the age of the church began (Acts 2). It was after this day that we first read of fasting in the community of believers called the church (Acts 13:1-3).

One day the Bridegroom will return and claim his bride, the church (Matthew 25:1-13; Ephesians 5:22-33). After this second coming, fasting will come to an end and the heavenly wed-ding feast will begin (Revelation 19:5-9). No more will the church be separated from the Groom. The marriage will commence and nothing will ever sever the bond (Revelation 21:1-22:5).

Until then, however, Jesus indi-cated that he expects his followers

> The fast of this age is not merely an act of mourning for Christ's absence, but an act of preparation for His return.... It will be a fasting and praying Church that will hear the thrilling cry, 'Behold, the Bridegroom!' Tears shall then be wiped away, and THE FAST be fol-lowed by THE FEAST at the marriage supper of the Lamb.[2]
>
> Arthur Wallis

to practice fasting. He even said that he would engage in at least a partial fast by not drinking from the fruit of the vine until he could drink it with his followers in the Father's kingdom (Matthew 26:29). That kingdom is here partially but not totally (Matthew 13:37-43; Luke 17:21). And it will not come in its fullness until the Son returns, establishes his earthly reign, and makes all things new (Revelation 19-22).

Since we know our Lord expects us to fast, let's return to learning more about this discipline and gaining some firsthand experience practicing it.

1. The reasons for fasting are as varied as the reasons for praying. The ways of fasting are, too. The Bible provides many examples that give us insight on both of these subjects.

   Read the passages cited below and fill the chart with the requested information wherever possible. While these texts do not cover all the Bible says about fasting, they provide plenty to ponder and draw upon for now.

	I Samuel 20:24-34	Nehemiah 1	Esther 3:8-15; 4:10-17	Luke 4:1-2	Acts 14:19-23
Who fasted?					
Why did they fast?					
How long was the fast?					
What were the dietary restrictions?					

Food-Fasting Exercise

2. Choose a day this week in which you can skip an entire meal. Feel free to drink water or juice during this time but nothing else.

   Regarding your reason for fasting, consider making it one

that at least loosely corresponds to a reason discovered in your study time above. Grief over a loss, repentance over a sin, remorse over someone's wrongful actions toward another, the selection and commission of spiritual leaders, preparation and protection for Satan's onslaughts or for someone else you are afraid to face—these are but a few of the many reasons you could choose for your one-meal fast.

Then, while you're fasting, use that time to take the reason for the fast to God in prayer. Speak to him silently or aloud about it, or write to him in your journal. This will make your time especially profitable.

Lifestyle-Fasting Exercise

3. Choose another lifestyle activity you can forego. If possible, make it a different activity from the one you chose last time. Then select a day this week you can abstain from this activity for a minimum of six consecutive hours.

Read step 2 above, the second and third paragraphs, to get the rest of the directions to follow during your fasting time.

▌Going Deeper

If you are *food* fasting, choose an additional day in which you can fast yet another meal, rather than fasting for just one meal on one day. So on two different days you will abstain from two different meals. You can retain the same purpose for the fast on both days or select a different purpose. Just remember the spiritual discipline of fasting should be practiced for spiritual reasons, not simply for earthly ones, such as losing weight or out of protest for a social cause or personal affront. Also, remember to combine prayer with your fast.

If your fasting concerns *lifestyle*, select an additional day this week when you can abstain from another activity for six consecutive hours. It can be one of the activities you have already fasted from or a new one. Make the reason for your fast the same or feel free to change it. Just keep your purpose for fasting spiritual, and join prayer to your fasting experience.

WEEK 8

When Less Is More

If anything can be found in abundance in our culture, it is food. There's fast food and fine food, deli cuisine and street vendor delicacies. You can have your food Mom's or Dad's way or Colonel Sanders' or McDonald's way. Your food can be to go, delivered, or eaten in the diner of your choice. You can bring it home from the store to be microwaved or cooked in the oven or on top of the stove. It can be eaten out of the can, bag, box, jar, or wrapper. You can take it with you and eat it standing up, sitting, exercising, traveling in your car, the subway, train, or airplane. With the horde of restaurants, vending machines, and mini-marts, you can get your food almost anywhere and any time of day or night. And we wonder why people in our society tend to be overweight. Since it's available, we eat it and eat it and eat it.

Contrast this with our Lord's attitude toward food. As a human being like us, in every way except for sin, Jesus got hungry and thirsty. His stomach could grumble and growl, and his mouth could become parched. He needed food and drink just like us, and he enjoyed feasting as well as anyone. He even said that he came "eating and drinking," in contrast to John the Baptist who "came neither eating nor drinking" (Mt 11:19, 18). John the Baptist's diet was sparse. It largely consisted of "locusts and wild honey" (Matthew 3:4). Jesus, on the other hand, attended wedding feasts, parties, and banquets where the food and wine flowed in abundance (Luke 5:29-30; John 2:1-10). Even some religious leaders of his day were disturbed at how much he and his disciples ate and drank when compared with John the Baptist and his followers who were known for their fasting (Matthew 9:14; Luke 5:30, 33). Jesus, it seemed, would eat with anyone, anywhere. Because of this, at least partially, he gained the reputation of being "'a gluttonous man and a drunk-ard, a friend of tax collectors and "sinners"'" (Mt 11:19).

Yet, on one occasion after Jesus and his disciples had been trav-eling much of the day, he stopped at a well for some water because he was tired and thirsty. While he waited at the well, his disciples went into the nearby town to buy some food. In the meantime, Jesus struck up a conversation with a woman who had come to draw water from the well. He asked her to draw some water for him to drink, and that launched them into a discussion about the difference between natural water that never quenches thirst for long and living water that satisfies spiritual thirst eternally.

When the disciples returned with the food, they found him with this woman. With their arrival, the woman left her water pot at the well and rushed back to town, telling the men to come out and see the man who could be the long-awaited Messiah. They came out of the city in droves looking for Jesus.

As the crowd came into view, the disciples tried to get Jesus to eat some of the food they had bought. But he would have none of it—not because he didn't need food or wasn't hungry, but because he knew that he was the food and drink these spiritually starved people craved. As he told his disciples, who still didn't seem to understand why he would not eat, "My food... is to do the will of him who sent me and to finish his work" (Jn 4:34). Jesus bypassed eating natural food so he could concentrate on passing out eternal food to the spiritually hungry. The result? Two days of productive ministry in which many townspeople came to believe that Jesus "really is the Savior of the world" (4:42).

Jesus loved to eat. He also loved to feed others. If in feeding others it meant at times that he would have to go without, so be it. His food was more than earthly; it was heavenly, too. His diet consisted of doing the Father's will. Often that included eating. Sometimes it meant putting up with a noisy stomach and a dry throat.

As followers of Christ, we need to have the mind of Christ in all things, including food. Like him, we can enjoy our food to the full. On the other hand, we need to realize that there are times when abstaining from eating is feasting on God's will. Fasting is not deprivation when it fulfills what the Lord desires. Our diet, like Jesus', should be a balanced mixture of the natural and the supernatural. An essential means to achieving that balance is the spiritual discipline of fasting.

> For the kingdom of God is not a matter of eating and drinking, but of righteousness, peace, and joy in the Holy Spirit, because anyone who serves Christ in this way is pleasing to God and approved by men.
>
> Apostle Paul
> (Romans 14:17-18)

DAY FIFTEEN

✍ Getting Started

The Bible depicts several different kinds of fasts.

- *Partial fast* —The diet is restricted (e.g., the amount or kinds of food may be cut down some), but no meals are missed.
- *Normal fast*—Nothing is eaten or drunk except water.
- *Absolute fast*—All food and liquid, including water, are removed from one's diet.
- *Supernatural fast*—This is an absolute or normal fast carried to the brink or even beyond the body's natural ability to sustain itself. The human body can normally go without water for three days and without food for twenty-one to forty days and still remain functional and close to borderline healthy. Past these periods, however, permanent damage can occur, including

death. The only way such harm can be avoided is if God miraculously sustains the fasting person.

This kind of fast is so rare and highly extraordinary that the Bible records only three occasions when this fast occurred (Deuteronomy 9:9; 1 Kings 19:8; Luke 4:1-2). Due to its miraculous, extremely rare, and dangerous nature, you should avoid engaging in this kind of fast unless God clearly and unequivocally directs you otherwise.[1]

The Bible also shows people fasting at various times.

- *Special need fasts*—These often occur in the face of emergencies, tragedies, egregious sins, intense periods of testing, or dramatic times of divine revelation or judgment. There's no regular liturgical occasion involved, just a special need.
- *Regular fasts*—These take place habitually. They might be weekly, monthly, or yearly, but they are always customary.

  Another element of fasting the Bible reveals concerns the number of people who fast and whether they do it privately or publicly.
- *Private fasts*—These are designed to keep the practice of the fast unnoticeable. The fasting individuals or group may go about their regular activities, but they do so in a way that veils the fact that they are fasting.
- *Individual fasts*—These are fasts carried out by one person, usually in private.
- *Group fasts*—These are fasts that usually involve low numbers of people committed to fasting for the same purpose. They can be private or public fasts.
- *Congregational fasts*—These are times when God's people gather as an assembly to fast. There's no attempt to hide the fact of their fasting from one another and perhaps even from the public at large.

- *National fasts*—These are public fasts engaged in by the populace of a city, region, or nation. The fasting is usually for some special need.

1. The following Bible passages present the sorts of fasts listed above. Look up each passage and determine which fasts are described. Write your answers in the spaces provided. Each space indicates a different type of fast.

Biblical Reference   **Types of Fasts**

Leviticus 16:29-34 ("deny _____   _____
yourselves" included
fasting; see Psalms 35:13)

Deuteronomy 9:9 _____ _____ _____

2 Samuel 3:31-35 _____ _____ _____

Ezra 10:6 _____ _____ _____

Daniel 1:5-16 _____ _____ _____

Daniel 10:1-3 _____ _____ _____

Joel 2:12-20 _____ _____

Jonah 3:1-10 _____ _____

Zechariah 8:19 _____ _____

Matthew 6:16-18 _____

Luke 2:36-37 _____ _____

Luke 18:12 _____ _____

Acts 9:1-9 _____ _____ _____

Acts 13:1-3 _____ _____

Acts 27:27-37 _____ _____ _____

Food-Fasting Exercise

2. Choose a day this week to try a lunch-to-lunch fast. This is a fast where on the first day you eat breakfast and lunch, then skip dinner. On the following day you skip breakfast, then break the fast by eating lunch. It's a one-day fast but only two meals are missed. Go ahead and take in liquids, but limit your drinks to water and fruit juices.

Remember, if you have a health situation that might prevent you from engaging in this kind of fast, then, if it is medically permissible, limit yourself to a partial fast from lunch to lunch.

When you fast this time, unless you have a more pressing need, commit your fasting time to your church community. Ask the Lord to accept your fast as an offering for your church's needs, ministries, and ministers. Use your body's calls for food as prompts to intercede on behalf of your church.

On the other hand, if you have a special need, wrap your time of fasting around that. As your study bore out above, fasting for special needs was a common practice in biblical times. The same has been so throughout church history. So if a greater need is there, apply the discipline of fasting to that.

Lifestyle-Fasting Exercise

3. If health reasons prevent you from practicing a food fast, give up a normal activity of your choice from noon on the first day to noon on the second day. Commit the fast to your church community or to a special need, as explained above under step two.

Going Deeper

Here are a few options based on food fasting. If you need to go with the lifestyle-fasting alternative, then simply adapt the following options accordingly. To go deeper into the discipline of fasting, try any one of these options, or choose any combination of the three.

1. If you are married to a believer, consider talking to your mate about abstaining from sexual relations for a time so you can fast and pray about your relationship and about your children (if you have them). (This is in keeping with Paul's counsel in 1 Corinthians 7:5.) Don't feel any pressure to engage in the fast this week or even next week. Choose a day or days that fit you both, then fast from lunch to lunch, and pray together and separately as often as you can.

   When your special prayer and fasting time ends, come together to discuss what the Lord impressed on your mind and heart during that time. You might want to use your journal to keep a record of what surfaces within you and between you as a couple during this period of abstinence and the times of discussion that follow.

2. If you have a close Christian friend, talk to him or her about joining with you in a partial or lunch-to-lunch fast. Discuss some of what you have learned about fasting, and select a

mutually agreeable time and reason to practice a fast. Encourage and pray for each other through the fast, then when the fast is over, get together to compare notes on your fasting experience and what you learned during it.

3. If you are a member of a prayer group or Bible study group, approach the members about committing themselves as a group to a time of fasting. Together select the time, the kind of fast, and the reason for fasting. When the fast is over, come together to talk and pray about what you learned. Let this fasting experience bring you closer together as a group and closer to God as your Lord.

DAY SIXTEEN
✍ Getting Started

1. Select any five biblical passages covered in the last day's exercises and read them with two questions in mind: What actions, if any, accompanied the discipline of fasting? What benefits, if any, came about as at least a partial result of the fast? You may need to read some of the larger context of each passage to answer these questions. In most cases, reading a few verses before or a few verses after will provide the answers you need.

   List the passages you choose in the left-hand portion of the column below, then place your answers in the remaining columns.

Bible Passages	Fasting Plus...	Fasting Benefits

Food-Fasting Exercise

2. Last time you fasted for your church community. This time broaden your vision to include your local community and perhaps even your county, state, and national officials. Focusing on these arenas, pick a day next week or the week after to fast at least one full day (abstaining from three meals) and maybe even two full days (skipping six meals). Combine the discipline of fasting with prayer and perhaps some other actions you observed in your Bible study these two weeks. During your fast, try limiting your liquids to water only. Drink only when you feel thirsty. Don't use water in an attempt to satisfy any hunger pangs you feel.

Lifestyle-Fasting Exercise

3. Choose an activity to forego, then adapt exercise two above to the practice of your fast.

Probing Further

If you want to explore engaging in longer food fasts—three-day fasts or longer—I encourage you to consult *God's Chosen Fast,* by Arthur Wallis, or *Celebration of Discipline,* by Richard Foster. These provide some excellent counsel on how to conduct longer fasts safely and productively.

Going Deeper

Rather than limiting fasting to times of special need or the Christian liturgical calendar, consider making it a regular habit. You might want to start by committing to a partial one-day fast or a full one-day fast once every two weeks. Whatever you decide to do, plan to do it for at least six months, maybe even for a year. After that time is up, assess how the fasts are going and what changes, if any, you would like to make in your practice of this discipline.

Your goal is to make fasting a normal part of your spiritual life, thereby reaping the many benefits its practice can bring into your private and public worlds. As Dallas Willard says in his classic work *The Spirit of the Disciplines:*

Persons well used to fasting as a systematic practice will have a clear and constant sense of their resources in God. And that will help them endure deprivations of *all* kinds, even to the point of coping with them easily and cheerfully.... Fasting teaches temperance or self-control and therefore teaches moderation and restraint with regard to *all* our fundamental drives. Since food has the pervasive place it does in our lives, the effects of fasting will be diffused throughout our personality. In the midst of all our needs and wants, we experience the contentment of the child that has been weaned from its mother's breast (Ps. 131:2). And "Godliness with contentment is great gain" (1 Tm 6:6).[2]

Get used to fasting. In the process you will learn to savor the divine food and drink that always satisfy.

WEEK 9

The Ministry of the Towel

"I have set you an example that you should do as I have done for you," Jesus said (Jn 13:15).

"Great, Lord. What did you have in mind? Do you want me to heal the sick and raise the dead as you did?"

"No, that's not what I meant."

"Well, then, how about telling great stories and preaching wonderful sermons? I can hold a crowd spellbound."

"I didn't mean that either."

"I know. You want me to stand up to corrupt government officials and religious leaders. In our day, we certainly have our share of those."

"You again missed my point."

"Then, Lord, tell me what example you set that I should follow? I'll do anything for you. Go on missionary treks to the remotest places of the earth. Demonstrate on picket lines and spend time in jail in support of the vulnerable and defenseless. I'll run for political office to initiate just social changes. Tell everyone I meet about the good news of salvation. Give all I own to feed the poor. You name it, I'll do it."

"All right, then. I want you to take a towel and basin of water and use them to clean the dirty, smelly feet of your fellow human beings."

"Yeah, right. You *are* kidding. I just know you are. After all, where's the ministry value in that? What lasting good will it do?

Their feet are just going to get dirty again. I'm interested in souls, not feet."

"Well, I am interested in whole persons, not just their souls. Why would I heal bodies and raise them from the dead if all I cared about were people's souls? I want you to wash feet so you will learn the essence and attitudes of service."

"Isn't there another way?"

"There is always another way."

"Great, what is it?"

"It is the way of selfishness, arrogance, pride, and rebellion."

"That sounds awful."

"It is more than awful. It is the pavement toward hell."

This imaginary dialogue builds upon a real event recorded in the Gospel of John. It is Jesus' last Passover meal. Jesus and the twelve disciples are in a room alone, and all of them have dirty feet. With unpaved roads and open sandals, dirty feet were a common feature in first-century Palestine. When guests arrived at a person's house, it was common for a servant to meet them at the door, remove their sandals, and clean their feet. If the owner of the house could not afford a servant, then one of the early arriving guests would accept the servant's role and wash the feet of the other guests. In this case, none of Jesus' disciples chose to take on what they must have seen as a demeaning task. So Jesus rose and took a towel and basin of water, then he stooped before each disciple and washed and dried his feet (John 13:3-5). "Jesus knew that the Father had put all things under his power, and that he had come from God and was returning to God" (v. 3). He was the royal King. Yet he exercised his cosmic status as the Ruler of all by kneeling before his creaturely subjects and cleaning their soiled feet.

When he finished washing the disciples' feet, he told them this: "You call me 'Teacher' and 'Lord,' and rightly so, for that is what I am. Now that I, your Lord and Teacher, have washed your feet, you also should wash one another's feet. I have set you an example that you should do as I have done for you. I tell you the truth, no servant is greater than his master, nor is a messenger greater than the one who sent him. Now that you know these things, you will be blessed if you do them" (vv. 13-17).

Do you want to teach as Jesus taught? Then teach as he served.

Do you want to preach as Jesus preached? Then preach as he served.

Do you want to evangelize as Jesus evangelized? Then evangelize as he served.

Do you want to lead as Jesus led? Then lead as he served.

Do you want to heal broken bodies as Jesus did? Then heal them as he served.

Do you want to do great things for God? Then do them as the God-man served.

Do you want to receive and enjoy God's blessings? Then serve as Jesus served.

Jesus is our example. And the example he gave us was

> For in self-giving, if anywhere, we touch a rhythm not only of all creation but of all being. For the Eternal Word also gives Himself in sacrifice; and that not only on Calvary. For when He was crucified He "did that in the wild weather of His outlying provinces which He had done at home in glory and gladness."... From the highest to the lowest, self exists to be abdicated and, by that abdication, becomes the more truly self, to be thereupon yet the more abdicated, and so forever. This is not a heavenly law which we can escape by remaining earthly, nor an earthly law which we can escape by being saved. What is outside the system of self-giving is not earth, nor nature, nor "ordinary life," but simply and solely Hell. [1]
>
> C. S. Lewis

servanthood. And the servanthood he showed us was the ministry of the towel. That means no act of service is too small for us, too dirty, too mundane, too menial, too trivial. Whether we are in the spotlight or the shadows, behind the pulpit or in the pews, receiving accolades or being overlooked, if we are serving others Christ's way, we are meeting needs for the sake of eternity. As we will see, some of these needs are even our own.

DAY SEVENTEEN
✍ Getting Started

Before we look into how to practice the discipline of service, let's get a firmer grip on what makes up true service.

1. Begin by meditating on the passages listed in the following chart. In the right column, jot down what you discover about the qualities of a Christian servant.

Scriptures on Serving	Qualities of a Christian Servant
Matthew 20:25-28	
2 Corinthians 3:4-5	
2 Corinthians 4:1-2, 5	
2 Corinthians 8:1-5	
Galatians 5:13-15	
Philippians 2:3-8	
Colossians 3:23-24	
Titus 3:1-2	
1 Peter 4:8-11	

2. Ask the Lord to show you what servant qualities need development in your spirit. Then, with your journal open and pen in hand, sit quietly before the Lord and wait for him to respond. Write what comes to your mind. Don't try to evaluate it, at least not yet. Just get it down on paper.

   If you run out of time or your journal entry remains blank, come before God later, repeat the request, and wait for his answer. Persistence in spiritual matters is a virtue. God will honor it.

3. When you complete the exercise, voice your gratitude to the Lord for answering your prayer. Then petition him to reward your pursuit of the servant's life by giving you a servant's heart and mind-set—the very qualities that marked Jesus as the Servant of servants. This is a request he fills with a smile. You may want to close your time with this prayer from Ignatius of Loyola:

> Teach us, Lord,
> to serve you as you deserve,
> to give and not to count the cost,
> to fight and not to heed the wounds,
> to labour and not to ask for any reward
> save that of knowing that we do your will.[2]

Going Deeper

Read the Gospel of Mark and note who Jesus serves, how he serves them, and how they respond to his service. This study will expand your understanding of what it means to serve as Jesus served.

DAY EIGHTEEN

Getting Started

In his book *Celebration of Discipline*, Richard Foster spells out the differences between true service and false service, humble service and self-righteous service. As we look to making the ministry of the towel a part of our lives, we would do well to keep these insightful observations in mind:

> Self-righteous service comes through human effort.... True service comes from a relationship with the divine Other deep inside....
>
> Self-righteous service is impressed with the "big deal." It is concerned to make impressive gains on ecclesiastical scoreboards.... True service finds it almost impossible to distinguish the small from the large service....
>
> Self-righteous service requires external rewards. It needs to know that people see and appreciate the effort.... True service rests contented in hiddenness. It does not fear the lights and blare of attention, but it does not seek them either....
>
> Self-righteous service is highly concerned about results. It eagerly waits to see if the person served will reciprocate in kind.... True service is free of the need to calculate results. It delights only in the service....
>
> Self-righteous service picks and chooses whom to serve....True service is indiscriminate in its ministry. . . .
>
> Self-righteous service is affected by moods and whims. It can serve only when there is a "feeling" to serve ("moved by the Spirit" as we say).... True service ministers simply and faithfully because there is a need.... The service disciplines the feelings rather than allowing the feeling to control the service.
>
> Self-righteous service is temporary. It functions only while the specific acts of service are being performed.... True service

is a life-style. It acts from ingrained patterns of living.

Self-righteous service is insensitive. It insists on meeting the need even when to do so would be destructive.... True service can withhold the service as freely as perform it. It can listen with tenderness and patience before acting.

Self-righteous service fractures community.... True service builds community.... It draws, binds, heals, builds.[3]

Let's turn to the practice of authentic, other-centered service in connection with family. Sometimes the hardest ones to serve are those closest to us. We know their shortcomings all too well, and they know ours, uncomfortably so. We also tend to take them for granted, just as they often do us. All the more reason for us to begin with them. Recall what Foster said. True service is not selective about whom it serves or whether it is applauded. It also seeks to bring people together rather than split them apart. Our families need to be built into genuine communities where grace and love abound. You can start that building program.

If you are single or have no children or living relatives, then adapt today's exercise to fit your relationships with friends, neighbors, or even work associates. There is always someone crossing your path who could use a good servant.

1. If you are in your home, take your journal and go into a family member's room. If you are away from your family and have pictures of them with you, pull those out and place them before you. What you're looking for is an object or setting that will connect you in a concrete way to your family.

2. Now look to the Lord to help you determine the needs of your family. Their needs will likely be multidimensional—spiritual, material, relational, psychological, medical, emotional, educational, volitional, vocational. Think about each family member and list each one's needs. You may need more time

> When people are hurting, they need more than an accurate analysis and diagnosis. More than professional advice. More, much more, than a stern, firm turn of a verbal wrench that cinches everything down tight.... Fragile and delicate are the feelings of most who seek our help. They need to sense we are there because we care... not just because it's our job.[4]
>
> Charles R. Swindoll

than you now have to do this. Take all the time necessary, even if it requires completing this step in chunks over the next several days.

I want to caution you to think not just in terms of meeting special, major needs, but also in terms of meeting the smaller, more routine needs. Let me illustrate what I mean.

- Make your family feel wanted with daily hugs and heartfelt compliments and praises.
- Let your spouse share her or his day at the office first, giving him or her your full attention and support.
- Keep a supply of your family's favorite cold drinks in the refrigerator.
- Encourage inquisitiveness by providing understandable answers, informative books, and outings to places of interest.
- Pray with and in front of your family, setting an example for what it means to depend on God.
- If you have a teenager harried by school, extracurricular activities, or a part-time job, give him a break from his household chores by doing them yourself for a week.
- Tuck notes of appreciation in lunch boxes and under pillows. We all need to feel special.
- Sit in silence with a hurting loved one who just can't talk

about his or her sorrow right now. Let your presence, arms, and tears convey your love.

- If your wife has been cooped up with your younger children for several days, surprise her with a full day off. You take care of the kids, the meals, and the housework. Let her do what she wants for the entire day.

- Perhaps travel or other circumstances frequently take you away from your family. Then liberally use the mail and telephone to stay in touch and express your devotion. Whenever possible, bring home mementos of your travels specially tailored for each family member.

- If you have family members unable to get out on their own, take them for car rides to beautiful settings or places that hold wonderful memories or the promise of fun. If they must remain homebound, then do what you can to bring beauty, humor, and joy to them.

3. With your list in hand, ask God to grant you wisdom and guidance on how those family needs can be met. Don't feel as if you have to handle them on your own. The Lord is with you, and there are probably other people who can come alongside you to service some needs more effectively than you can. Serving sometimes means standing aside and allowing others to meet the needs. My family knows I can fix small things around the house, but major jobs require more expertise and skill than I have. So I serve them by bringing in someone else to do the work I cannot. Similarly, you may have a family member who needs trained psychological counseling or vocational advice beyond your abilities to supply. Be humble and caring enough to find other people who can satisfy that need. If you can't think of someone, ask other people if they can. Keep God in the loop also. Several times he has brought people across my path without my ever mentioning the need to anyone but him.

4. Now begin serving. The best way to learn is to do. I suggest you start with something small. Not an act that will make a big splash, just send a ripple. You want to cultivate the discipline of true service. For most of us that requires beginning with almost invisible tasks, ones that may go unnoticed for a while, certainly ones we do not announce or look to draw attention to.

As you move out, do yourself a favor. Be patient with yourself. The learning process is always fraught with more mistakes than successes, at least at first. Don't let that discourage you. Expect it, learn from it, and press on. Remember your example, Jesus Christ. Even he "learned obedience from what he suffered" (Heb 5:8). If he had to go through a sometimes painful learning curve, how much more should we expect to. Thankfully, we can count on him to be with us and enable us through every bump and pothole along the way. How wonderful is our Teacher!

Going Deeper

One way to nurture the inner spirit of service is through "flash prayers."[5] While with your family or thinking about them, silently pray for them. Keep your prayers brief: "Lord, deepen your joy in my daughter"; "Father, show my wife your faithfulness"; "Holy Spirit, let your peace settle my husband's nerves." Your service will be hidden, but its fruit will soon flourish all around you.

WEEK 10

Neighbor-Love

If we are to serve as Jesus served, we must obey the commandment to love our neighbors as we love ourselves (Matthew 22:39; Leviticus 19:18). But who is our neighbor? Whom should we love and therefore serve? An expert in interpreting the Old Testament Law asked Jesus about this, and he answered by telling the man a story (Luke 10:29-37). You have likely heard this story; it's called the parable of the Good Samaritan. What many Christians do not realize is how shocking the story was to first-century Jews. Indeed, once we probe into the depth of this simple-sounding narrative, we will see how much it shakes our world as well.[1]

The Opportunity

Jesus tells about a man who was traveling from Jerusalem to Jericho. He doesn't tell us who this man was. His identity—name, family background, nationality, race, vocation, education, religious beliefs—is left completely open. Moreover, to ensure his identity can't be learned, Jesus says that thieves fell upon him and robbed him, stripped him of all his clothing, beat him until he was "half dead," then left him to die (vv. 30-31). In the Middle East, travelers can discover a person's ethnic and religious orientation by his (or her) manner of dress or speech. Just a quick glance at his clothes or a few words from his mouth are often all it takes to tell what region and religious community he calls home. So when Jesus said this man's clothes were taken, he left him unidentifiable. Jesus made matters even worse by saying the traveler was left "half dead." These words mean next to death or at the point of death. This state would have left the man unconscious, therefore unable to tell anyone who he was. So with his clothing and other belongings gone and his ability to speak taken, too, the man was reduced to a mere human being in desperate need.

Jesus does not specify some other details his hearers would have naturally supplied. For example, first-century travelers knew that the road between Jerusalem and Jericho was seventeen miles of dangerous territory. The road descended sharply and "curved through rugged, bleak, rocky terrain where robbers could easily hide"[2] and regularly did. While there were many hiding places near the road, much of the road itself could be easily seen for long distances. Travelers coming along the road from either direction could see fellow travelers quite far away. One man who has traveled this road, as well as many other "Middle Eastern roads by camel, by donkey, and on foot for twenty years," remarks, "I know that the traveler is *extremely* interested in who else is on the road. His life may depend on it. A question put to a bystander at the edge of the last village just before the desert begins; a brief exchange with a traveler coming the other way; fresh tracks on the soft earth at the edge of the road where men and animals prefer to walk; a glimpse in the clear desert air of a robed figure ahead; all these are potential sources of knowledge for the... traveler."[3] This means that other travelers may have seen a scuffle in the distance and approached the area with heightened interest and caution.

Priestly Neglect

Jesus says that the first traveler to come along was a priest (v. 31). Priests were part of the upper class. As aristocrats, they didn't walk seventeen miles between Jerusalem and Jericho, as the poor did. They rode on animals, such as donkeys. So riding along a priest comes to the place where he may have seen a fellow traveler jumped, and he sees the man beaten and lying still near the roadway. The priest doesn't help the man at all. He doesn't even come near him. In fact, he goes out of his way to avoid him by moving to the opposite side of the road and continuing on his way.

The priest could have tended to the man's wounds and used his mount to carry the victim to safety and a place where he could receive long-term care. Yet the priest refused. Why, Jesus doesn't say. Perhaps the priest feared being ambushed by robbers himself. He may have also been protecting himself from being defiled. The man was unconscious, after all, and could have been dead. The priest knew from the written law that touching a corpse would make him unclean, and therefore make it impossible for him to carry out his duties until he had become ritually purified again (Numbers 19:11-22). If it turned out that the man was not a Jew, whether he was dead or alive, the priest would have been regarded as unclean, too. According to the oral Jewish law of the day, the second most unclean act was contact with a Gentile. Touching a corpse was first on the list. The priest may have been more concerned with avoiding sin, proving his commitment to the law, or maintaining his work and travel schedule than with reaching out to a man in obviously critical straits. Whatever the priest's motive, Jesus makes it clear that he failed to act out of love.

A Levite Takes Leave

The next passerby was a Levite (Luke 10:32). Priests served in the temple, offered sacrifices, and collected, distributed, and ate tithes. Levites assisted priests by taking care of the temple and performing a variety of other administrative tasks. Jesus says that a Levite came upon the same spot in the road where the wounded, naked man lay. Jesus' language indicates that the Levite not only saw the injured man but got close to him before turning away and leaving him.

Once again, Jesus does not say why the Levite did not help the man. In all likelihood, the Levite saw the higher-ranking priest pass by the victim. This may have led him to conclude that since the priest saw no duty to help the man, who was he to question the priest's judgment by helping the stranger himself? Such an act might offend the Levite's superior, challenging not only the priest's interpretation and application of the law but also his affection for fellow human beings. The Levite may also have been afraid of being defiled by a dead man or jumped by robbers, though probably less so than the priest since he made the riskier move of getting close to the injured man. Despite the reason for neglect, the Levite leaves the man for dead and goes on his way. Another chance to act lovingly is missed.

Samaritan Service

The third traveler to come down the road was a Samaritan (v. 33). Jesus' listeners would have expected this person to be a Jewish layman. The progression would have been perfect: priest, priestly assistant, layman. All three classes of people had jobs to do in the Jerusalem temple. If they were leaving Jerusalem after the daily temple sacrifices held there, one would expect to see representatives of all three classes on the road out of town. Instead, Jesus rocks the world of his Jewish audience by introducing a Samaritan.

Jews hated Samaritans. The Mishnah, a collection of written laws considered by many Jews to be second in authority only to the Hebrew Scriptures, declares, "He that eats the bread of the Samaritans is like to one that eats the flesh of swine."[4] A contemporary Bible scholar notes that the "Samaritans were publicly cursed in the synagogues; and a petition was daily offered up praying [to] God that the Samaritans might not be partakers of eternal life."[5] The animosity between Jews and Samaritans was centuries old by Jesus' day. They despised one another and often went out of their way to avoid one another. They saw each other as enemies. And yet, the Samaritan was not viewed as a Gentile. To Jews he was a heretic but not a non-Jew. He, too, accepted the five books of Moses as Scripture, though he rejected the rest of the Hebrew canon as authoritative. He also believed in worshiping one God, but held that Shechem rather than Jerusalem was the true site of worship.

So along comes a hated Samaritan, traveling through Jewish territory where doctrinal orthodoxy reigns. He has likely seen the priest and Levite on the road, and probably noticed how they crossed to the other side at a certain point. When he reaches that same juncture, he sees the wounded stranger, goes near him, and, unlike the Jewish priest or Levite, feels tremendous compassion for him (v. 33). The Samaritan may fear for his safety and ritual purity as the priest and Levite did. However, he does not let that deter him from rendering aid. Instead he cleans and softens the man's wounds with oil, disinfects them with wine, then binds them so they will stay clean and better heal (v. 34).

Oil and wine were standard first-aid remedies in the ancient world. Priests also used them in connection with sacrifices in the temple worship. In Jesus' parable, the Samaritan uses the elements of ritual sacrifice in an act of personal sacrifice. He gives of himself and his own resources, even though one would expect the priest and Levite to do that. You see, the priest and Levite were regularly reminded of the value of sacrifice since they officiated twice daily at sacrificial offerings in the temple. For whatever reason, though, they failed to make the connection between ritual sacrifice and personal sacrifice. So in Jesus' story the theologically orthodox are heretical in practice, while the theological heretic is orthodox.

As if this were not bad enough, Jesus inflames his audience even further. He adds that the Samaritan gave his own mount to the injured man and took him to an inn. There he took care of the man for the rest of the day, then paid the innkeeper to watch after him while he completed his journey. The Samaritan promised to return and settle any more bills that might have accumulated as a result of caring for the anonymous man

(vv. 34-35). Good thing, too. Stripped of his belongings, the stranger lacked the ability to pay his bills. If he could not pay, he would not be permitted to leave. He might even find himself arrested and sent to debtors' prison (see Matthew 18:23-35). The Samaritan foresees this problem and solves it.

The Samaritan's actions are not only sacrificial but courageous. In Middle Eastern society, acts of blood-revenge were common. If family members believed someone had killed a loved one, they would seek to kill that person. If they could not find him, they had the right to retaliate by killing any members of his family, then any family relation no matter how remote, and finally any member of his tribe. By taking the wounded man to an inn, the Samaritan put his life in danger. He ran the grave risk that someone in the stranger's family would recognize him and assume that the Samaritan was responsible for his injuries. Who else is there to blame?

> The group mind of Middle Eastern peasant society makes a totally illogical judgment at this point. The stranger who involves himself in an accident is often considered partially, if not totally, responsible for the accident. After all, why did he stop? Irrational minds seeking a focus for their retaliation do not make rational judgments, especially when the person involved is from a hated minority community.... An American cultural equivalent would be a Plains Indian in 1875 walking into Dodge City with a scalped cowboy on his horse, checking into a room over the local saloon, and staying the night to take care of him. Any Indian so brave would be fortunate to get out of the city alive *even* if he had saved the cowboy's life. So with the Samaritan in the parable, his act of kindness will make *no* difference. Caution would lead him to leave the wounded man at the door of the inn and disappear. The man may still be unconscious, in which case the Samaritan would be completely protected. Or the Samaritan could remain anonymous to the

wounded man. But when he stays at the inn through the night to take care of the man, and promises to return, anonymity is not possible.[6]

By the time the parable ends, the Samaritan is the indisputable hero. He has reversed with kindness every act perpetrated against the injured stranger:

The Thieves	The Samaritan
Rob him	Pays for him
Beat him	Binds his wounds
Leave him dying outside	Leaves him cared for inside
Abandon him	Promises to return

The Priest and Levite	The Samaritan
Pass by him	Goes to him
Show him no mercy or love	Shows him sacrificial mercy and love

The Real Question

The story told, Jesus asks the expert in the law, "Which of these three do you think was a neighbor to the man who fell into the hands of robbers?" (Lk 10:36). Notice Jesus does not re-ask the question the legal expert posed, namely, Who is my neighbor? He rejects the question. To Jesus, the real question is not, "Who is my neighbor?," but, "What kind of neighbor must I be?" The real issue concerns the one who should love and the extent that love should be shown. Once that's settled, the answer to "Who is my neighbor?" is simple: Everyone, including my enemies! Neighborly love has no limits. Jews can love Samaritans, and Samaritans can love Jews. Not race, nationality, religious beliefs, social status, physical condition, or any other factor can set any limits on authentic neighbor-love. We must love whoever crosses our path. That is the uncompromising demand of love.

The legal expert gets the point but cannot bring himself to say the word *Samaritan*. Instead he answers that the real neighbor was "the one who had mercy" (v. 37). Jesus then tells him, "Go and do likewise" (v. 37). Imagine, Jesus telling a Jewish expert in the Mosaic Law to follow the example of an unorthodox, hated Samaritan. Amazing. Certainly boundary-shattering. And definitely humanly impossible.

Only God can overcome our prejudices and help us love more as we ought. We can never satisfy the demand of love, but the One who is love can. As we depend on him in obedience, he will perfect our love and love others through us (1 John 4:7-12, 16-21). Love comes from God. It is revealed as part of the fruit of the Spirit (Galatians 5:22). So by serving the divine Lover, we can bring his love to bear on the lives of others. What a wonderful gift he gives us! What a wonderful gift he allows us to give to others!

DAY NINETEEN
✍ Getting Started

The Samaritan loved a stranger who was in desperate straits and could not repay his kindness. That's the kind of sacrificial service we will focus on today.

1. Needy people reside in each of our communities. We don't have to look to other cities or countries to find people who could use someone's help, though there's nothing wrong with doing so.

   More than likely, you have heard about some people who need a neighbor's touch. They may live on your street, across town, or even farther away. Perhaps they are widows or orphans, unwed mothers or confused fathers. Maybe they are recovering from surgery and have no one to care for them once they leave the hospital. They might be homeless or in danger of losing their homes. Whatever their situation, they are hurting and hungry for love.

Without considering anything else about them other than their need, come up with some ways you can touch their lives. Think about what you have to give that will help. Move beyond the idea of simply mailing them a check. Think instead in terms of your talents, time, spiritual gifts, emotional investment... those things that involve sacrificial self-giving.

2. If you don't know of anyone who needs help, contact a local soup kitchen for the hungry, a shelter for runaway kids or unwed mothers, a safe house for abuse victims, a hospital, or local jail house. Many churches also have ministries to needy folks. You may want to contact your church first to see what you can do to serve. Believe me, you should have no trouble finding hurting people.

3. Another option you may want to consider is to start a ministry out of your own resources. For example, during my musician days, I pulled together local professional musicians and got them to commit to spending several hours per week giving private or group music lessons to the poor. In many cases, the music instruction was free. When we charged, our fees rarely rose higher than ten dollars for four lessons a month. Music stores sometimes supplied instruction books and used instruments for our students at drastically reduced rates. At times we bought the music for our students and managed to find them free instruments. In our own small way, we gave young, disadvantaged people hope and beauty in worlds they usually found bleak.

> Let every day therefore be a day of humility; condescend to all the infirmities of your fellow-creatures, cover their frailties, love their excellences, encourage their virtues, relieve their wants, rejoice in their prosperities, compassionate their distress, receive their friendship, overlook their unkindness, forgive their malice, be a servant of servants, and condescend to do the lowest offices to the lowest of mankind.[7]
>
> William Law

4. If you are homebound for some reason, pray and fast (via food or life style) for the needy. If you can, write letters of encouragement and hope, or use your phone to reach out to the hurting. We can all find ways to love and serve, whatever our personal situation.

5. Finally, as you go about your daily business, keep your eyes and heart open. Who knows, you may be traveling down a road someday and come across a suffering stranger, much like the Good Samaritan did. Don't pass by. Stop and help. Remember, the discipline of service is a sacrificial lifestyle, not an occasional event. Neighbor-love is boundless.

Going Deeper

The greatest love you can show another person is to introduce her (or him) to the Savior. You don't have to be a full-time evangelist to do that. You just need to be willing to open your life to others, to tell them about the hope you have in Christ Jesus and how they can have that hope as well. You don't need a manual to show you how to do this. You simply need to be a neighbor. Give freely of yourself, including sharing with others the divine Lover who motivates and guides you. He will handle the rest.

DAY TWENTY

✍ **Getting Started**

One of the toughest lessons in the parable of the Good Samaritan is that loving service includes service to our enemies. Even in straight instruction, Jesus made this uncomfortably clear:

Love your enemies, do good to those who hate you, bless those who curse you, pray for those who mistreat you. If someone strikes you on one cheek, turn to him the other also. If someone takes your cloak, do not stop him from taking your tunic. Give to everyone who asks you, and if anyone takes what belongs to you, do not demand it back. Do to others as you would have them do to you.

If you love those who love you, what credit is that to you? Even "sinners" love those who love them. And if you do good to those who are good to you, what credit is that to you? Even "sinners" do that. And if you lend to those from whom you expect repayment, what credit is that to you? Even "sinners" lend to "sinners," expecting to be repaid in full. But love your enemies, do good to them, and lend to them without expecting to get anything back. Then your reward will be great, and you will be sons of the Most High, because he is kind to the ungrateful and wicked. Be merciful, just as your Father is merciful. LUKE 6:27-36

In this passage, Jesus reiterates that neighbor-love must be shown toward those who mistreat us. He also provides the answer to a question people often ask: "If I love my enemies, how can I keep them from taking advantage of me?" Jesus' response: "They may very well take advantage of you. You are free not to worry about that. Just love them. Leave the rest to my Father. He will take care of the situation and reward you."

Jesus is not talking here about throwing caution to the wind. Some people are just outright dangerous and destructive. We should protect ourselves and our families from undue harm. At the same time, we can still find ways to show love to the unmerciful and wicked. How we do that will vary with the circumstances, but that we do it should remain a constant in our lives.

1. Today I want you to consider how you can show love to someone who has mistreated you. I realize this may be terribly difficult to do. It may even seem impossible. Jesus said, "What is impossible with men is possible with God" (Lk 18:27). I know from experience that this is true. God can show you its truth, too, but you must trust him.

2. Begin by trying to see people as God does. They bear God's image, no matter how faint that image may seem at times. That means the individual has inherent value and worth in God's eyes.

   He or she is also a person for whom Christ died and rose from the dead. The gospel applies to him or her as much as to anyone.

   People who strike out at others are like wounded animals—they know they are in pain but they resist attempts others make to relieve that pain. In fact, by fighting against those who wish to help, aching people bring even more pain upon themselves. Their pain may be loneliness or emptiness. Perhaps they're struggling to make ends meet, but pride gets in the way of their accepting assistance. Maybe they are afraid. Maybe they have been so scarred by other people that they distrust everyone. Reflect deeply on this person's situation to see if you can arrive at some understanding of what may be causing her or his pain.

3. Commit this struggling person to prayer. Not only pray for him or her but pray for healing in your attitude toward this person. Ask the Lord to help you see how you can be a Good Samaritan in this person's life.

4. Once you have in mind what you're going to do, go at it sensitively and in a caring manner, and leave your expectations at home. Things may go well or fall apart. You may melt a heart or encounter granite. Achieving certain results should not be your aim. Just love. Give the ministry of the towel—that's all you're after. The rest is up to God.

> You must learn not to be upset over an injury because it is an offense to you. Rather, out of your love for God, train your thoughts on the harm that your enemy is doing to his own soul with each sin or offense he commits.
>
> Then it will become easier for you to show your love for this "enemy" by responding not out of anger but in godly kindness.[8]
>
> Francis of Assisi

Going Deeper

Sometimes we create enemies by our own actions. We dirty the reputations of others or betray their confidence. We speak to them condescendingly or embarrass them. We have hundreds, yea thousands, of ways to turn people against us.

For the next several days apply your study skills to your interactions with other people. Like a crime detective searching for clues, look for signs of relational espionage. What might you be saying or doing that is putting people off? Keep in the front of your mind what bothers you, then maintain a watchful eye to see if you behave in those ways. Chances are you do, and you're not even aware of it.

Pay particular attention to your tongue. "With the tongue we praise our Lord and Father," writes James, "and with it we curse men, who have been made in God's likeness.... My brothers, this should not be" (Jas 3:9-10). Listen carefully to yourself. Are you tearing people down or building them up? Are you encouraging them in the Way or leading them astray? Try countering every negative thing you say by saying something positive. Cultivate noble, pure, praiseworthy speech. Let your words become like cool, spring rain falling on parched, neglected ground.

WEEK 11

The Pursuit of Purity

My parents were deeply devoted to the Christian faith, and they raised me in that faith. I was baptized as an infant, went to church every Sunday, and was active in the church youth group. In my preteen years, I sang in the choir and served as an acolyte. When there was a youth retreat, I was there. Christian camps and their routines were familiar scenes to me.

Of course, church and camps were not my only sources of Christian education. My mother sang hymns around the house and with my father conducted family devotions in the weeks leading up to Easter and Christmas. My folks also taught me to pray each day, and they frequently drew attention to the Bible's relevance in handling life's diverse concerns.

I grew up surrounded by people who believed in a God who had spoken and mattered. For the most part, I enjoyed it all. But it was not until I was nineteen that I gave myself to him who is life.

At the time I was dating a teenager named Pamela who would later become my wife. I was playing drums in my church's many music groups, and each week I would hear the familiar refrains of how to enter into a personal relationship with Jesus Christ. I knew who Jesus was, and I knew all about the gospel. I could have told the evangelical story to anyone by heart. The problem was that this story had not become my story. I was a character in a different book. I wanted to change stories, but I wanted to do it my way. I felt dirty inside, not just ritually but morally unclean. I had no doubt I was a sinner, and I knew that Jesus came to save sinners. Still, for a reason I could not explain at the time, I decided that I had to clean up my own life before turning it over to Christ. Bizarre, isn't it? I desperately needed and wanted forgiveness. However, I also believed I could make myself a forgiveness-free zone. I would come to Jesus purified, and the purifier would be me. So Sunday after Sunday I would hear the altar call to accept Christ by faith. And each time I would feel a tug of war within, something urging me to go forward while I fought back to remain in my seat. I always won the conflict by convincing myself that Jesus really didn't want me just as I was but only as I could be.

One Sunday evening, an evangelist came to our church and presented the gospel message in a way that shattered my misconceptions. I don't want you to misunderstand me. This man shared the same message I had always heard about the way to Christ. The difference came in his ability to knock down the barriers I had erected across that road to Christ. One by one my barricades fell. I sat transfixed by this man, hanging on his every word, amazed that he seemed to be talking only to me. How could he know? I had never told anyone. I thought, in fact, that everyone believed I was a genuine Christian. I knew I was not. My sin overwhelmed me. Guilt and shame polluted and ate away at my soul. I felt like a tiger caught in the teeth of a steel trap. I hurt and wanted to escape, but the trap was too strong. My attempts to free myself had all ended in greater pain and despair.

When the evangelist sat down and the altar call began, the war within me raged as it never had before. This time the inner compulsion to respond swept over me. The pull to step out of the pew and into the aisle was tremendous but not overwhelming. I knew I had a choice. On the other hand, I also believed that if I did not go forward I never would. I had hit a dead end. I could stay in the cul-de-sac of my sin and pride, or I could turn around and run toward unconditional love and forgiveness and finally find freedom. The choice quickly dissolved to one liberating option, and I took it.

I left my seat next to Pamela, went to the front of the church, and walked into the room reserved for respondents. It was the same room that often served as a center for music group practices. I didn't care about that now. All I wanted was Christ.

A choir member followed me into the room and sat next me. Together we began to pray. I fell on God's mercy and confessed my sins. Within what seemed like seconds tears were streaming down my cheeks and neck. With them my guilt and shame rushed out of my soul as if they were being chased.

Soon my tears of remorse turned to tears of release. An inexpressible joy welled up inside, filling every crevice of my soul, binding every wound sin had inflicted. I was free. FREE! Christ was in me. I was in him. My liberator had delivered on his promise. Egypt was behind me. The Promised Land loomed ahead. I was on the way home and determined never to look back.

I also quickly discovered that I would have cherished companions in my journey. Sitting several seats away from me was Pamela. She, too, had given her life to Christ and found the freedom of forgiveness. Next to her sat my sister, Carol, also a new creation in Christ. Close to Carol were my parents. They had renewed their faith-commitment to the Lord. What a grace-filled night it was. Confession truly is good for the soul.

DAY TWENTY-ONE

✍ Getting Started

Freedom in Christ begins with confession. It also remains and expands with confession. The Christian life is a confessing life. Without acknowledging our sin before God and depending on

> ... We are good ontologically. God didn't make junk, and we still bear his image, however defaced....
>
> But though ontologically we are very good, morally we are not. We are sinners. Our world is a battlefield strewn with broken treaties, broken families, broken promises, broken lives, and broken hearts. We are good stuff gone bad, a defaced masterpiece, a rebellious child..[1]
>
> Peter Kreeft

his mercy to purge it from our lives, freedom will always elude us, and guilt and shame will constantly plague us. Developing the discipline of confession will keep the polluters at bay and deepen the transforming work Christ began in us when we placed ourselves by faith in his merciful hands. Confession, in other words, is a means for pursuing purity.

Before we take a closer look at confession, let's get a sobering view of sin. To really appreciate what confession does for us, we need to see what sin does *to* us. The picture isn't pretty, but it's one we must look at with solemn realism.

1. To begin with, the popular sentiment that to err is human is false, if by *err* one means "sin." Sin is an alien force, an invader, a parasite. God did not create it, and he did not make it a part of human nature. When he created the first human beings, he declared them and the rest of the created order "good" (Genesis 1:31)—not a mixed bag of good and evil, just good. Sin entered human history later, and it came because of human disobedience (Genesis 3).

This means that since sin is not a part of who we are, by banishing the invader from our lives we will find restoration, completion. Our humanity will be enhanced, not diminished.

Sin is the destroyer. It eats away at our humanness; it defaces the divine image. Sin is not us. We are sinners, yes. But sin is unhuman, unnatural. It is an obscene distortion that deserves only to be shattered. With it smashed to pieces, we will find wholeness.

2. So you can see this yourself, look up the following Bible passages on sin, and summarize what they say under the appropriate categories. Under "Sin's Nature" place descriptions and synonyms of sin (e.g., unrighteousness, disobedience, transgression); under "Sin's Extent" jot down whom sin has affected; under "Sin's Ways" put the manifestations of sin (violence, pride, immorality, etc.); and under "Sin's Wages" note sin's real payoff, not the lies it promises.

A Biblical Portrait of Sin

Scriptures on Sin	Sin's Nature	Sin's Extent	Sin's Ways	Sin's Wages
Romans 1:18				
Romans 2:5-9				
Romans 5:12				

Scriptures on Sin	Sin's Nature	Sin's Extent	Sin's Ways	Sin's Wages
Romans 6:23				
Romans 7:13-23				
Galatians 5:19-21				
2 Thessalonians 1:6-9				
James 1:13-15				
James 2:8-11				
1 John 3:4				

3. Sin. What is it good for? Absolutely nothing! Its mission is seek and destroy, and it works to accomplish that relentlessly and mercilessly.

4. For the rest of your time, even over the next few days, reflect on what these passages say about sin. Ask the Lord to sensitize you to sin's pervasive, corrupting presence in your public and private worlds. Make some form of fast part of your sensitizing exercise. Pour out your findings in your journal, no matter how dirty and ugly they may be. The goal is to strip sin of its veneer of false promises and pseudo pleasures and really see it for what it is.

I realize this assignment seems extremely negative, but that's just an appearance. It is really quite positive, at least that is the direction in which it leads. For when we see the seriousness of our illness, we are much better prepared to hear and heed the cure.

✓ Checking In

Some people have very sensitive souls, souls often damaged by abuse or tragedy. These people question everything they do. They find no value within themselves. Worth is measured by performance only, and their performance never measures up. Consequently, they come to despise themselves. In numerous ways they undermine their own lives. "Self-destruct" is the sentence written across their hearts, and they sometimes carry it out with brutal effectiveness.

If this describes you, even only partially, you run the risk of turning the Bible's teaching on sin into added justification for your self-hatred. What you need to come to know in your spirit is how incredibly valuable you are in God's eyes. You are not a worm or a useless cog. You are God's adopted child, his precious jewel, his wondrous image-bearer. He has made you incomparably unique and so pregnant with worth that he paid the highest price possible to win you back—his very own Son.

I urge you to ask the Lord to show you daily how much he loves you. I also encourage you to seek the help of a professional Christian counselor, someone who can help you see how valuable you truly are and show you how to overcome the messages inside that seek to destroy you. Finally, I would like to recommend some books worthy of your time. These are resources many other individuals have found helpful and comforting in their struggle with self-worth: *Healing Grace*, by David A. Seamands (Wheaton, Ill.: Victor, 1988); *Measuring Up*, by Kevin Leman (Old Tappan, N.J.: Revell, 1988); *Perfect Every Time: When Doing It All Leaves You with Nothing...*, by Paula Rinehart (Colorado Springs, Colo.: NavPress, 1992); *Shame and Grace: Healing the Shame We Don't Deserve*, by Lewis B. Smedes (San Francisco: Harper San Francisco/Zondervan, 1993).

DAY TWENTY-TWO
✍ Getting Started

Today we're going to turn from studying our disease to learning about its cure—a much more delightful task.

1. In his first epistle, the apostle John exhorts Christians to live in the light of their new life in Christ: "This is the message we have heard from him [Jesus Christ] and declare to you: God is light; in him there is no darkness at all. If we claim to have fellowship with him yet walk in the darkness, we lie and do not live by the truth. But if we walk in the light, as he is in the light, we have fellowship with one another, and the blood of

Jesus, his Son, purifies us from all sin" (1 Jn 1:5-7).

Does this mean Christians never sin? No. However, it does mean that sin will not characterize our lives. John is emphatic about this. If we call ourselves Christians and keep living as if we are not—that is, if sin reigns over our lives rather than righteousness and love—then we are not truly Christians (1 John 3:4-20). Holy living and charity accompany saving faith (Galatians 5:6; James 2:14-26). The notion that a sin-riddled, loveless faith obtains everlasting life is nonsense as far as Scripture is concerned.

So what should we do when sin gains the upper hand? How can we beat it back? Confess it, John says: "If we confess our sins, he is faithful and just and will forgive us our sins and purify us from all unrighteousness.... My dear children, I write this to you so that you will not sin. But if anybody does sin, we have one who speaks to the Father in our defense—Jesus Christ, the Righteous One. He is the atoning sacrifice for our sins, and not only for ours but also for the sins of the whole world" (1 Jn 1:9; 2:1-2). When we confess our sin, our heavenly Defense Attorney goes to work pleading our case. With him for us, who can stand against us? The Father always hears his Son out, and the Son always speaks and does his Father's will. Talk about having the Judge's ear! How can we miss?

2. The apostle John's instruction in this matter is so important that you need to give it a closer look. Check out 1 John 1:9 and 2:1-2 again. With those passages before you, answer these questions as a way of getting to the heart of these texts:

What does God want us to do when we sin? _____

_____

What does he promise to do when we obey him? _____

_____ .

What is it about him that leads him to do this for us? _____

_____ .

What role does Jesus play in this process? _____

_____ .

3. Well, then, since confession is the means to overcoming sin's corrupting impact, you need to understand what confession involves. In Scripture and subsequent reflections on its teaching, Christians have come to recognize four characteristics of confession:

a. **We admit we have sinned.** We face the fact that we have disobeyed God. Self-justifications, rationalizations, and excuses of all sorts and sizes are laid aside. We call our wrongdoing what it is—a violation of God's perfect, all-good standards.

b. **We acknowledge our sin.** Specifics, not vague generalities, are the hallmarks of confession. "Lord, when I shouted at and berated my son this morning, I sinned against you and him." "Father, I know I lied in that meeting yesterday. I was trying to cover my tracks and save face, which were also acts of dishonesty."

c. **We are sorrowful over our sin.** Like rust eating the metal away on a car, sin corrodes whatever it contacts. When we serve sin rather than holiness, we become agents of corrosion (Romans 6:11-23). We corrupt ourselves, other people, the environment, and most importantly, our relationship with God. This should grieve us. It should lead us to abhor our sin, to regret deeply that we have offended the Lord and caused so much damage. In biblical times, people often expressed their sorrow over sin by cries of lament, fasting, tearing their garments, or wearing sackcloth and pouring ashes over their heads. They took sin seriously. Today we may express our remorse in different ways, but we dare not be flippant about our transgressions. When our sin puts a smile on our face rather than repels us, we have no sorrow.

d. **We determine to avoid sin.** True confession creates in us a yearning for holy living. We want more of God. We want to drink and eat just at his table. Our cravings turn away from the paltry offerings of sin and feed off the superabundance of Jesus Christ. No other feast will do. We are in the banquet hall of the King. Why leave to eat at the insect-infested, rundown inn at the edge of town when we can have our eternal fill of the finest delicacies in royal surroundings? We have tasted the best, and we want to savor it and have more. We do not want sin to ruin the feast anymore, not even a single dish, not even a single bite.

4. Now that you know what confession involves, begin the process of prayerful, honest self-examination. Are there sins you need to confess? If any surface, you might want to take a piece of paper separate from your journal and jot them down. Then confess them to God and find forgiveness in him. Remember, fasting can be a way of communicating your sorrow over your sin. Let this discipline play a healing role in the confession process.

When you've taken your sins before God and laid them at the footstool of his throne, take the piece of paper with your list of sins, tear it into tiny pieces, and throw it in the trash. Let that act symbolize what God has done for you in response to your confession. As the psalmist so eloquently expresses it:

> Praise the LORD, O my soul;
>   all my inmost being, praise his holy name.
> Praise the LORD, O my soul,
>   and forget not all his benefits—
> who forgives all your sins
>   and heals all your diseases,
> who redeems your life from the pit
>   and crowns you with love and compassion,
> who satisfies your desires with good things
>   so that your youth is renewed like the eagle's.
> … The LORD is compassionate and gracious,
>   slow to anger, abounding in love.
> He will not always accuse,
>   nor will he harbor his anger forever;
> he does not treat us as our sins deserve
>   or repay us according to our iniquities.
> For as high as the heavens are above the earth,
>   so great is his love for those who fear him;
> as far as the east is from the west,
>   so far has he removed our transgressions from us.
> As a father has compassion on his children,
>   so the LORD has compassion on those who fear him.…
>
> PSALMS 103:1-5, 8-13

5. Now go and enjoy your freedom to live in obedience to him. In the power of his Spirit, strive for the high call of holiness. "As obedient children," the apostle Peter exhorts, "do not conform to the evil desires you had when you lived in ignorance. But just as he who called you is holy, so be holy in all

you do; for it is written: 'Be holy, because I am holy'" (1 Pt 1:14-16).

Also remember, should you sin again, confess it and move on. Don't let sin control or subvert you. With Christ as your Advocate, the Spirit as your Power, and the Father as your Lover, sin is completely out-matched. The victory is yours, as long as you persevere in the Light.

Going Deeper

If you can, take your Bible and steal away to a place of quiet and solitude. Once you are situated, turn to the Old Testament and read 2 Samuel 11:1-12:25. This section of Scripture records the events surrounding King David's adultery with Bathsheba and the fallout of his sin. Then read Psalm 51, a song of confession penned by David after his sin had been revealed. Together these

The command 'Be ye perfect' is not idealistic gas. Nor is it a command to do the impossible. He is going to make us into creatures that can obey that command. He said (in the Bible) that we were "gods" and He is going to make good His words. If we let Him—for we can prevent Him, if we choose—He will make the feeblest and filthiest of us into a god or goddess, dazzling, radiant, immortal creature, pulsating all through with such energy and joy and wisdom and love as we cannot now imagine, a bright stainless mirror which reflects back to God perfectly (though, of course, on a smaller scale) His own boundless power and delight and goodness. The process will be long and in parts very painful; but that is what we are in for. Nothing less. He meant what He said.[2]

C. S. Lewis

passages provide a telling portrait of the lure of sin, the cost of sin, and the mercy God shows to the penitent.

Meditate on these texts with your own situation in mind. Let them cast light on any darkness lurking within. Use them to give courage to your will to avoid sin's enticements and thereby its exacting price. Allow them to convince you ever more thoroughly that God is serious about eradicating sin from the lives of his children.

WEEK 12

Forgiveness Unlimited

There once was a man who had two sons. They were a well-to-do, Middle Eastern Jewish family living two millennia ago.

One day the younger son came to his quite healthy, vibrant father and demanded that he divide the inheritance between him and his older brother. Then, to add insult to injury, the younger son pressured his father to grant him full disposition rights of his share of the inheritance so he could sell it.

The son's actions were an outrage. They were tantamount to telling his father that he wanted him to die. He had no legal right to make his demands, and there existed no custom to support him either. In fact, his requests had never been made anywhere in the Middle Eastern world before. His acts were unthinkable and intolerable. Certainly fathers were allowed to, and often did, divide their property between their children before their death, especially when their health was failing. They would do this to avoid the eruption of family disputes after they were gone. Even in this case, though, fathers would retain disposition rights or in another way secure income from the property so they could meet their own needs during their lifetime. Sons knew this. They would not think, much less try, to violate their fathers' right to earn a living from the fruit of their toil. But this younger son did not care about his father. Whether his father lived or died, ate or starved made no difference to him. All he wanted was his inheritance and the ability to use it as he pleased—now. His father could sink into Sheol for all he cared.

The village residents would have expected the father to beat his son and throw him out of the house permanently and penniless. At the very least, they would have expected the father to give his son a verbal licking and severely discipline him. Indeed, it would have been within the father's rights to take similar action with his older son. After all, it was the older son's duty to protest his brother's selfish, improper demands and to work to reconcile his brother to his father. He just stood there, though, and remained silent. He simply waited to see what his father would do. This, too, told his father that his older son wished him dead. How much this must have hurt the father. Imagine the depth of the insult and hatred he must have felt from both his sons. What would he do?

This father startled everyone by giving in to his son's demands. He divided his holdings between his two sons and gave the younger sibling the right to dispose of his share as he wished. The older son observed the transaction and accepted knowledge of his share without even a hint of protest. He was every bit as disloyal toward his father as his younger brother was.

On his part, the father demanded nothing in return. He didn't even fly into a rage. His gentle, loving treatment of his sons was in stark contrast to their coldhearted acts.

Well, the younger son didn't dawdle. He went into the village and passed from buyer to buyer, selling off his inheritance for traveling currency. As word spread about his ill treatment of his father, the community's horror and hatred intensified. What would have normally taken months to sell, the young man managed to barter away within days. No doubt he wanted to escape the condemning looks and growing rejection of the villagers he knew so well.

Soon he was gone. His newfound wealth in tow, he traveled to a faraway land where Jews were few and Gentiles were plentiful. There he squandered his entire inheritance in wasteful living.

About that time a famine began ravishing the land. Jobs were scarce and money was running low. The young man became desperate and attached himself like glue to a citizen in this foreign land. During difficult times, the indigent frequently threw themselves on the mercy of potential benefactors. When a benefactor wanted to rid himself of these beggars, he would assign them tasks he believed they would refuse. This young man's newfound savior was no exception. He told the destitute Jew to go out to the fields and feed the pigs. To Jews, pigs were unclean animals. The man, no matter how bad off, should have turned up his nose and walked away. Instead he became a pig herder. In fact, he was so famished, he longed to eat the bitter berries off the shrublike plants fed to the pigs. If he had, it would not have benefited him. These berries lacked the nourishment needed to meet a human being's needs. Much to his chagrin, he soon discovered that the food given him for his work was insufficient, too. He could not stave off his hunger. He knew he was slowly starving to death.

As he considered his desperate straits, he finally realized that he had exhausted his resources. He would soon die if he didn't take a different course. While thinking about the home he left, he remarked to himself, "How many of my father's hired men have food to spare, and here I am starving to death!" So he concocted a plan: "I will set out and go back to my father and say to him: 'Father, I have sinned against heaven and against you. I am no longer worthy to be called your son; make me like one of your hired men'" (Lk 15:17-19). He wasn't really ashamed of how he had treated his father. His only sin, he thought, was squandering his inheritance—a sin for which he would ask his father's forgiveness.

If his father went for his plan, the young man could save face, for the most part anyway. He would be a hired servant, therefore a free man, not a slave. And he would have his own income and the means to live independently in the village. His social status, then, would be fairly equal to his father's. He would be able to maintain his pride and sense of self-sufficiency. With the money he earned, he could also repay his father and by that compensate for the money he lost. Furthermore, since he would not be living in his father's house, he would not have to seek reconciliation with his brother. In short, his plan would allow him to work and buy his way out of his dilemma without restoring any family relationships.

The worst glitch in his plan was the expected reaction of the townspeople and extended family members. His relatives would likely cut him off completely, and the rest of the village would take out their pent-up hostilities on him for insulting his father, selling his inheritance, losing it to Gentiles, and humiliating himself and other Jews by herding pigs. He saw no way past this problem. The larger community would just have to be faced and endured.

So, he set off toward home.

As he approached the village, his father spotted him, and compassion welled up within him for his son. He knew the townspeople would badly treat his Prodigal Son. They would certainly abuse him verbally, perhaps even physically. So he rushed through the village toward his oncoming son. Residents were stunned to see this nobleman, with his long-flowing robes, running down the street. Men of such high standing never ran in public. They walked slowly, with pomp and dignity. Why would this man humiliate himself so?

The answer was quickly apparent. In an act of incredible compassion and superlative love, this father ran up to his wayward son, threw his arms around him, and kissed him on the cheek repeatedly. Villagers ran to the scene and gazed in shock. This was the son who had despised his father, who had wished him dead. Yet the father had embraced him as if he had done no wrong. What other staggering gestures of unconditional acceptance would they see?

The son began his prepared speech: "Father, I have sinned against heaven and against you. I am no longer worthy to be called your son" (v. 21).

But before he could finish, the father turned to his servants, who had finally caught up to him, and shouted with joy, "Quick! Bring the best robe and put it on him" (v. 22). This was the father's finest robe, the one reserved for feast days and great cele-brations. By giving it to his son to wear, the father was assuring the community that he accepted his son without reservations and that they should do the same. "Put a ring on his finger," the father added (v. 22), indicating his remarkable trust of his son. Then he told his servants to put sandals on his son's feet—an irrefutable sign that the servants were to treat his son as a mem-ber of the family, not as a servant. He, like his father, was to be regarded as a master in the house.

The overjoyed father also called for an all-out celebration: "'Bring the fatted calf and kill it. Let's have a feast and celebrate. For this son of mine was dead and is alive again; he was lost and is found'" (vv. 23-24). So with the father, his fully accepted son, and their servants, the townspeople walked joyfully through the streets, spreading the news about the great party that would soon take place at the nobleman's house.

The son never finished his speech and never carried out his plan. His father's profound outpouring of love led him to humbly accept forgiveness for his sins. Grace won. He entered his father's house a beloved son, not a servant or a hired hand. Now freed from his past failures, he could join his father and make merry.

What a merry time it was! To devour a fatted calf required more than a hundred people with ravenous appetites. The village adults poured into the house, and the musicians among them began to play. People danced, sang, and clapped so loudly that the field hands far away heard the commotion and came to join in. The nobleman's older son came, too. He had been in the fields with the hired hands, directing their work.

As he got closer to the house, he noticed all the children out-side. While not allowed inside with the adults, the children joined in the celebration outside. They danced and sang along with the music and played games. The older son came up to one of the partying boys and asked him what was going on. When the boy told him, he was furious. He refused to go in the house and join the revelry. He knew that custom required his presence. His father and the villagers would expect him to mingle, to make sure everyone had enough to eat, to offer compliments, and to keep the servants at the peak of their performance as they waited on all the guests. But he wanted none of it.

Somehow, his father learned that he was outside and quite bent out of shape. So again, this great nobleman humbled himself, came out to his older son, and pleaded with him in front of the children and gathering guests to join the party. But his son became hostile and chose to embarrass and insult his father by quarreling with him publicly.

"Look!" his son indignantly blurted out. "All these years I've been slaving for you and never disobeyed your orders" (v. 29).

Why is he referring to himself as if he were a servant or hired hand? we can hear the father say to himself. *Doesn't he realize he's my very own son?*

"Yet you never gave me even a young goat so I could celebrate with my friends" (v. 29).

How can he be so selfish? He has the run of the house and access to all I have. Why is he disputing with me as if he were a laborer haggling over wages?

"But," continued the insolent son, "when this son of yours who has squandered your property with prostitutes comes home, you kill the fattened calf for him" (v. 30).

Now he has publicly insulted his own brother by exaggerating his sin with this charge of carrying on with harlots. How can I get him to understand how much I love him? How can I also help him see his younger brother as I see him?

"My son," the father finally said with endearment and a tone seeking reconciliation, "you are always with me, and everything I have is yours. But we had to celebrate and be glad, because this brother of yours was dead and is alive again; he was lost and is found" (vv. 31-32).

Once again, the father showed his deep, abiding love for his son and his willingness to humble himself to make that love known.

His guests were stunned—twice in a single day. What unexpected devotion, they murmured. What grace and mercy!

In case you didn't recognize it, this is the parable of the Prodigal Son told by Jesus in Luke 15:11-32. I expanded it based on what Bible scholars know about first-century life in the Middle East.[1] I brought out several cultural facts and word meanings that show the power and ongoing relevance of this story.

As you can see, this is a story about unconditional love in the face of blatant, egregious sin. Both sons wish their father dead by their actions. Both sons insult and embarrass their father. Both of them show how self-centered and ungrateful they are. And yet, their father responds to them with unselfish love and deep compassion. As the master of the house, he becomes a servant to his sons, humiliating himself before them and the rest of the community in order to win them. Although both sons ask to be treated as servants, their father treats them as sons. They, of course, can spurn his fatherly love. Jesus tells us that the younger son did not, but he leaves the issue open when it comes to the older son. We don't know if the older son accepted his father's overtures of love and grace. We do know, however, that the invitation is always there for all people—not always from an earthly father, perhaps, but always from our heavenly Father.

God's arms are waiting to embrace us and bring us home as sons and daughters, loved and honored forever. We may be squandering our lives far away from home, or we may be near the house living as servants in rebellion. To our heavenly Father, where we sin doesn't matter. What does is that we accept his humble, grace-filled invitation to enter his house forgiven and restored and there join the celebration already in progress. His home is filled with sinners such as ourselves—fellow sons and daughters who disobeyed him and lost their way. They returned confessing their sin and admitting their need. He rushed out to greet them, clothed them in his finest raiments, and escorted them home. As the apostle John reminds us, "If we confess our sins, he [God] is faithful and just and will forgive us our sins and purify us from all unrighteousness" (1 Jn 1:9).

Are you willing to accept his grace-filled love?

DAY TWENTY-THREE

✍ Getting Started

While all sin is ultimately against God, many of our transgressions are also against other people. As we sin vertically, we often sin horizontally. What should we do when we are the offending party?

1. Jesus tells us what to do in Matthew 5:23-24. Look up this passage and write down the four steps we ought to take.

Step 1: _____

_____ .

Step 2: _____

_____ .

Step 3: _____

_____ .

Step 4: _____

_____ .

2. Does someone have something against you? Have you wronged a person? Is there a strained or broken relationship because of your sin? Prayerfully and humbly follow Jesus' counsel. Go to that person. If at all possible, go personally so you can meet face to face. If the physical distance between you both is too great, then call the offended party by phone. If that's out of the question, then contact the person by letter or electronic mail. Find a way to reach him or her. Then seek forgiveness and reconciliation. Do what you can to set things right.

   With the human relationship restored, turn heavenward and ask the Lord to forgive you too. He will, you know. Of that you can be sure.

3. In his book *Improving Your Serve*, Charles Swindoll mentions several problems you might face as you seek reconciliation, and he suggests ways to handle them. I pass these on to you:

   "But what if he or she won't forgive [me]?"... The important thing for each of us to remember is that you are responsible for *you* and I am responsible for *me*. With the right motive, in the right spirit, at the right time, out of obedience to God, we are to humble ourselves... and attempt to make things right. God will honor our efforts. The one offended may need time—first to get over the shock and next, to have God bring about a change in his or her heart. Healing sometimes takes time....

   "What if the situation only gets worse?"... This can happen. You see, all the time the one offended has been blaming you... mentally sticking pins in your doll... thinking all kinds of bad things about you. When you go to make things right, you suddenly cause his internal scales to go out of balance. You take away the blame and all that's left is the person's guilt, which does a number on him, resulting in even worse feelings. But now it's no longer your fault....

... "What if it is impossible for me to reconcile because the offended person has died?"... In such unique cases, I recommend that you share your burden of guilt with someone whom you can trust. A close friend, your mate, a counselor, or your pastor. Be specific and completely candid. Pray with that individual and confess openly the wrong and the guilt of your soul. In such cases... prayer and the presence of an understanding, affirming individual will provide the relief you need so desperately.[2]

Going Deeper

Confession, of course, is not just needed for outward offenses. We can sin against God and other people in our hearts and thoughts. Jesus made this point when he stated: "You have heard that it was said, 'Do not commit adultery.' But I tell you that anyone who looks at a woman lustfully has already committed adultery with her in his heart" (Mt 5:27-28). The same is true with the commandment not to murder. Those who violate it will be judged by God, as will those who harbor anger against others (vv. 21-22). Bitterness, hatred, lust, vengeance, heartlessness, envy, greed, neglect, betrayal—these are just a few of the condemnable acts we can commit without even so much as raising our voices at anyone else. We carry them through in our minds or savor them in our hearts; that is wickedness enough.

As you go through your days, pay close attention to the workings within you. When the unethical slips from the fleeting to the dwelling upon, from innocent imaginings to flights of evil fancy, understand you have interior sin that needs divine forgiveness and purging. Get radical with it (vv. 29-30). Do what it takes with the Spirit's assistance to rid its influence from your life experience.

You are in a spiritual war with wickedness. You can't make

peace with sin, and you can't overcome its power on your own. You must stand fast against it and fight it with spiritual weapons (Eph 6:10-18). The ultimate victory is yours in Christ, but the war will go on until he comes again and vanquishes his enemies forever (1 Corinthians 15:24-28; Revelation 19-20). He will protect you and fight with and for you. Nevertheless, the battles will be easier if you refuse to give sin even a toehold in your life.

DAY TWENTY-FOUR

Getting Started

Last time we looked at what to do when we were the offenders. Today we want to consider how to handle offenses against us.

1. Ponder the introduction to this chapter, the story about the Prodigal Sons. You may want to look up Luke 15:11-32, which is the Bible passage that presents this parable. What does the father's behavior tell you about how you should respond to people who sin against you? Jot down your conclusions in your journal.

2. Now turn to Matthew 18:21-35, and read what Jesus says about forgiveness. How often should you forgive those who offend you? Why should you be so forgiving? How important are your acts of forgiveness in God's sight? Again, record your answers in your journal. Keep in mind also that by forgiveness Jesus means hurling our resentment far from us so it will no longer hold any influence over us.[3]

3. With this biblical teaching before you, write down the names of any individuals toward whom you harbor resentment. They may have offended you recently or a long time ago. Next to

their names, note what they did and, as best you can, why you have not forgiven them.

4. Now turn your thoughts toward your heavenly Father. Consider the high cost he paid to redeem you and how fully he has forgiven you. You may want to read Psalms 103:1-14.

5. Finally, return to your list of offenders and offenses and take each item before the Lord in prayer. Confess your hatred and resentment. Fast as an expression of your sorrow. Ask the Lord to help you forgive those who have hurt you so deeply. It may take hours of prayer and fasting over days or many months before you can really say that you have forgiven each person from your heart. How will you know when forgiveness has begun? You will know *"when you recall those who hurt you and feel the power to wish them well."*[4]

Let today be your first step toward the healing process. In time you will see the incredible freedom and joy forgiveness brings. That's *his* promise to us, and he always keeps his promises.

▼ Going Deeper

You may have wounds that run so deep that the idea of forgiveness seems like a cop-out. You can't imagine turning away from your anger and canceling the sentence of payment you've passed against your offender. The sin was too great, the pain too intense. The offender deserves to be punished. If anything, you want to pray for his (or her) demise, at least that he receive a just punishment for his crime.

Don't ignore these feelings. Like the pain that throbs around a fresh wound demanding medical attention, your inner hurt calls out for attention, too. It may need psychological or psychiatric care. It certainly needs to be tended by the divine Physician. And like any serious wound, it will need a lot of care and plenty of time to heal.

First, however, you must realize that your affliction requires attention not revenge or simply justice. History is replete with people who exacted revenge or brought the guilty to justice and still died with gaping, internal wounds. Because they never applied the balm of forgiveness to themselves, their bitterness plagued them and eventually destroyed them.

Second, you probably need to consider seeking help for your pain. A pastor or a professional Christian counselor would be a good start.

Third, I would suggest that you read a book by Lewis Smedes entitled *Forgive and Forget: Healing the Hurts We Don't Deserve*. It is the most honest and compre-

Suppose you never forgive, suppose you feel the hurt each time your memory lights on the people who did you wrong. And suppose you have a compulsion to think of them constantly. You have become a prisoner of your past pain; you are locked into a torture chamber of your own making. Time should have left your pain behind; but you keep it alive to let it flay you over and over.

Your own memory is a replay of your hurt—a videotape within your soul that plays unending reruns of your old rendezvous with pain. You cannot switch it off. You are hooked into it like a pain junkie....

The only way to heal the pain that will not heal itself is to forgive the person who hurt you. Forgiving stops the reruns of pain....

You set a prisoner free, but you discover that the real prisoner was yourself..[5]

Lewis B. Smedes

hensive book on forgiveness I have ever read, apart from the Bible.

Last, and definitely not least, I urge you to take your pain daily before the Wounded Healer himself. Let him work in even the deepest recesses of your wounds. He knows what to do, and he knows how deeply you hurt. No one has ever been ravaged by sin more than he has. Jesus Christ went so far as to become sin for us as he hung on the cross (2 Corinthians 5:21). He took what we deserved on himself (1 Peter 2:24-25). Because he paid our debt, "CANCELED" is now written across even the most vile sin we have ever committed against God (Colossians 2:13-14). Because of Christ, we can stand before God completely forgiven.

What he did for us, he can do within us. He can bring us to the point where we can forgive from our hearts the sins committed against us. This is love's ultimate power. When it's unleashed, chains fall, walls crumble, and people are reconciled to one another and to the Lord.

Give him a chance. Let him in. What do you have to lose? Only the hate that imprisons and the bitterness that poisons.

✓ Checking In

You made it! Although you are a busy Christian, you managed to work through this book and begin practicing six spiritual disciplines of the deeper life. Congratulations! You have eaten at the table of countless Christians who have gone before you. You have tasted traditional dishes that may have been new to you, perhaps others familiar but in some ways made fresh. I hope you enjoyed the meals, though some may have been difficult to swallow.

Now you have another choice to make. You can return to the table of inwardness and take larger helpings of the dishes of discipline. You can keep feeding your soul the nourishment it so desperately needs. Or, you can return to a starvation diet. Like the son who wasted his inheritance and nearly died of hunger, you, too, can squander the wealth you have in Christ and end up lusting after the world's slop. The choices are as stark as life and death, heaven and hell. There is no third way. C. S. Lewis had it right: "Aim at Heaven and you will get earth 'thrown in': aim at earth and you will get neither."[6] If you want the best of both worlds, heaven must be your focus.

An appendix follows: it contains resources you can use to sharpen your study skills, especially those relating to the study of Scripture. Do yourself and your loved ones a favor. Keep digging deeper into the depths of Scripture and the spiritual disciplines. Pick up some books mentioned in the appendix. Delve into them and taste what they have to offer. Their offerings are good, I know; I've tasted them myself. I believe you will find your palate satisfied too.

Now go. Draw nourishment from the table of our Lord. Use the disciplines to train yourself for the endurance race of faith. Stay the course. Keep running the race. Reach for the gold. Then when the race is over, you will be able to say, "It is finished. I have run the race set before me and crossed the finish line. The victory is mine." And he will meet you on the winner's platform. There, before throngs of other believers, he will turn to you and give you an imperishable crown. Then you will hear the words every creature longs to hear from his Creator, "Well done, good and faithful servant. Now enter my rest and enjoy the overflowing abundance of Paradise."

Come, Lord Jesus, come.

APPENDIX

Resources for Bible Study

A wide range of study resources is available in the area of biblical studies. I have taken the liberty to mention a handful of resources that are user-friendly for beginning Bible students. These are mostly Protestant in orientation, since that is the Christian tradition in which my convictions largely reside. However, for the most part, these resources are also committed to much of the classical Christian understanding of the faith as articulated by such theologians as Augustine, Anselm, and Aquinas. In that light, Roman Catholic and Eastern Orthodox Christians should also find this material beneficial.

Bible Dictionaries

Youngblood, Ronald F., ed. *Nelson's New Illustrated Bible Dictionary.* Nashville, Tenn.: Nelson, 1995.

Douglas, J.D. et al., eds. *New Bible Dictionary,* 2nd ed. Downers Grove, Ill.: InterVarsity Press, 1982.

Lexical Tools

Brown, Colin, ed. *The New International Dictionary of New Testament Theology,* 4 vols. Grand Rapids, Mich.: Zondervan, 1976. Those unfamiliar with linguistics will have trouble with these volumes. A knowledge of Greek is not needed, though it is helpful.

Rienecker, Fritz. *Linguistic Key to the Greek New Testament.* Edited by Cleon L. Rogers, Jr. Grand Rapids, Mich.:

Zondervan, 1980. A knowledge of Greek is unnecessary to use this resource.

Harris, R. Laird, Gleason L. Archer, Jr., and Bruce K. Waltke, eds. *Theological Wordbook of the Old Testament*, 2 vols. Chicago: Moody Press, 1980. Students with a fair understanding of linguistics will be able to use these volumes. These books are keyed to *Strong's Exhaustive Concordance*, making it unnecessary for users to have a working knowledge of Hebrew.

Vine, W. E. *An Expository Dictionary of Biblical Words.* Edited by Merrill F. Unger and William White. Nashville, Tenn.: Nelson, 1985. This resource is especially easy for beginning students to use.

Bible Atlases

Beitzel, Barry J. *The Moody Atlas of Bible Lands.* Chicago: Moody Press, 1985.

Jenkins, Simon. *Bible Mapbook.* Belleville, Mich.: Lion, 1985.

Blaiklock, E.M., ed. *The Zondervan Pictorial Bible Atlas.* Grand Rapids, Mich.: Zondervan, 1972.

Manners and Customs

Gower, Ralph. *The New Manners and Customs of Bible Times.* Chicago: Moody Press, 1987.

Packer, J.I., Merrill C. Tenney, and William White, Jr., eds. *Nelson's Illustrated Encyclopedia of Bible Facts.* Nashville, Tenn.: Nelson, 1995.

van der Woude, A.S., ed. *The World of the Bible.* Grand Rapids, Mich.: Eerdmans, 1986.

Archaeology Resources

Millard, Alan. *Treasures from Bible Times.* Belleville, Mich.: Lion, 1985.

Blaiklock, E.M. and R.K. Harrison, eds. *The New International*

Dictionary of Biblical Archaeology. Grand Rapids, Mich.: Zondervan, 1983.

Old Testament History and Overviews

Bruce, F. F. *Abraham and David: Places They Knew.* Nashville, Tenn.: Nelson, 1984.

Walton, John H. *Chronological and Background Charts of the Old Testament.* Grand Rapids, Mich.: Zondervan, 1978.

Wood, Leon. *A Survey of Israel's History.* Grand Rapids, Mich.: Zondervan, 1970.

New Testament History and Overviews

Bruce, F. F. *Jesus and Paul: Places They Knew.* Nashville, Tenn.: Nelson, 1981.

Green, Joel B. and Scot McKnight, eds. *Dictionary of Jesus and the Gospels.* Downers Grove, Ill.: InterVarsity Press, 1992).

Hawthorne, Gerald F. and Ralph P. Martin, eds. *Dictionary of Paul and His Letters.* Downers Grove, Ill.: InterVarsity Press, 1993.

Tidball, Derek. *The Social Context of the New Testament: A Sociological Analysis.* Grand Rapids, Mich.: Zondervan, 1984.

Dealing with Controversial Passages

Archer, Gleason L. *Encyclopedia of Bible Difficulties.* Grand Rapids, Mich.: Zondervan, 1982.

Brauch, Manfred T. *Hard Sayings of Paul.* Downers Grove, Ill.: InterVarsity Press, 1989.

Bruce, F. F. *The Hard Sayings of Jesus.* Downers Grove, Ill.: InterVarsity Press, 1983.

Geisler, Norman, and Thomas Howe. *When Skeptics Ask: A Popular Handbook on Bible Difficulties.* Wheaton, Ill.: Victor, 1992).

Stein, Robert H. *Difficult Passages in the New Testament: Interpreting Puzzling Texts in the Gospels and Epistles.* Grand Rapids, Mich.: Baker, 1990.

NOTES

The Race:
Discipline and the Deeper Life

1. Commentators and theologians disagree about the nature of this reward. I am inclined to agree with those who see it as one of special service and privilege in the future kingdom life planned for believers (see Matthew 25:14-23; 2 Corinthians 5:10-11; Revelation 5:9-10; 7:14-17; 22:3, 12). I think it is a divinely bestowed reward based on what believers do with what they receive from God. If they draw on his resources and use them well, he will reward them. If they use his resources sparingly and poorly, he will not reward them even though he will save them. In my understanding, the reward is for service rendered, not for the gift of salvation.

   Just as a reward can be gained, so it can be lost (Matthew 25:24-30; Colossians 2:18; 2 John 8; Revelation 3:11). Paul did not want to be disqualified for his reward of service, which is why he trained vigorously and ran resolutely (1 Corinthians 9:24-27).

   To get a sense of the breadth of belief on the matter of reward in Scripture and Christian theology, see Jerome D. Quinn, "The Scriptures on Merit," in *Justification by Faith: Lutherans and Catholics in Dialogue, VII*, H. George Anderson, T. Austin Murphy, and Joseph A. Burgess, eds. (Minneapolis, Minn.: Augsburg, 1985), 82-93; Joseph A. Burgess, "Rewards, But in a Very Different

Sense," in *Justification by Faith*, 94-110; "Recompense, Reward, Gain, Wages," in *The New International Dictionary of New Testament Theology*, edited by Colin Brown (Grand Rapids, Mich.: Zondervan, 1978), vol. 3, 134-45; Lewis Sperry Chafer, *Major Bible Themes*, rev. by John F. Walvoord (Grand Rapids, Mich.: Zondervan, 1974), 281-86; Charles Hodge, *Systematic Theology* (Grand Rapids, Mich.: Eerdmans, 1979, reprint), vol. 3, 231-45.

2. Jerry Bridges, *The Practice of Godliness* (Colorado Springs, Colo.: NavPress, 1983), 263.

3. Bridges, 42.

4. Dallas Willard, *The Spirit of the Disciplines: Understanding How God Changes Lives* (San Francisco: Harper & Row, 1988), 68.

5. Rick Yohn, *Beyond Spiritual Gifts* (Wheaton, Ill.: Tyndale House, 1976), 165.

ONE: *Prayer*

Week One

1. Richard J. Foster, *Celebration of Discipline: The Path to Spiritual Growth*, revised and expanded ed. (San Francisco: Harper & Row, 1988), 33.

2. Peter Kreeft, *Prayer: The Great Conversation* (Ann Arbor, Mich.: Servant, 1985), 19.

Week Two

1. Henri J. M. Nouwen, *The Way of the Heart* (New York: Ballantine, 1981), 60.

2. M. Basil Pennington, *The Manual of Life: The New Testament for Daily Living* (Mahwah, N.J.: Paulist, 1985), 8.

TWO: *Study*

Week Three

1. C. S. Lewis, *Letters of C. S. Lewis*, as cited in Wayne Martindale and Jerry Root, eds., *The Quotable Lewis* (Wheaton, Ill.: Tyndale House, 1989), 408, para. 1008.
2. C. S. Lewis, *The Four Loves* (New York: Harcourt Brace Jovanovich, 1960), 176.
3. Augustine, *Letter 137*, 3, as quoted in John E. Rotelle, ed., *Augustine Day by Day* (New York: Catholic Book Publishing, 1986), 18.

Week Four

1. Howard G. Hendricks and William D. Hendricks, *Living by the Book* (Chicago: Moody Press, 1991), 227.
2. Philip S. Watson, comp., *The Message of the Wesleys*, as quoted in Bob Benson and Michael W. Benson, *Disciplines for the Inner Life* (Nashville, Tenn.: Generoux/Thomas Nelson, 1989), 121.
3. Colin Brown, ed., *The New International Dictionary of New Testament Theology*, 4th ed. (Grand Rapids, Mich.: Zondervan, 1975), s.v. "Father," vol. 1, 615.
4. Fritz Rienecker, *A Linguistic Key to the Greek New Testament*, ed. Cleon L. Rogers, Jr. (Grand Rapids, Mich.: Zondervan, 1980), 17-18.

THREE: *Journaling*

Week Five

1. Henri J. M. Nouwen, *¡Gracias!: A Latin American Journal* (San Francisco: Harper & Row, 1983), 16, 18, 58.
2. Nouwen, *¡Gracias!*, xiii.

3. Gordon MacDonald, *Ordering Your Private World* (Chicago: Moody Press, 1984), 146.
4. Elizabeth O'Connor, *Letters to Scattered Pilgrims*, as cited in Bob Benson and Michael W. Benson, *Disciplines for the Inner Life* (Nashville, Tenn.: Generoux/Thomas Nelson, 1989), 133.

Week Six

1. Madeleine L'Engle, *Walking on Water: Reflections on Faith and Art* (Wheaton, Ill.: Harold Shaw, 1980), 137.
2. MacDonald, 141.
3. The following list of questions was inspired by a similar list given by Howard and William Hendricks in their book *Living by the Book* (Chicago: Moody Press, 1991), 305-7.

FOUR: *Fasting*

Week Seven

1. Willard, 166.
2. Arthur Wallis, *God's Chosen Fast: A Spiritual and Practical Guide to Fasting* (Fort Washington, Penn.: Christian Literature Crusade, 1968), 26.

Week Eight

1. God never calls on people to practice a fast that would endanger their health. In the three biblical instances where a supernatural fast occurs, there is no indication that the individuals involved (Moses, Elijah, and Jesus) were in any danger. God took care of their bodily nourishment needs miraculously. We do not know how he did this, but we know he did. As pastor Donald Whitney states, "These [fasting occasions] required God's super-

natural intervention into the bodily processes and are not repeatable apart from the Lord's specific calling and miraculous provision." (Donald S. Whitney, *Spiritual Disciplines for the Christian Life* [Colorado Springs, Colo.: NavPress, 1991], 153).

2. Willard, 167-68.

FIVE: *Service*

Week Nine

1. C. S. Lewis, *The Problem of Pain* (New York: Macmillan, 1962), 152.
2. Ignatius of Loyola, "Dedication," in *The Living Testament: The Essential Writings of Christianity Since the Bible*, M. Basil Pennington, Alan Jones, and Mark Booth, eds. (San Francisco: Harper & Row, 1985), 224.
3. Foster, 128-30.
4. Charles R. Swindoll, *Growing Strong in the Seasons of Life* (Portland, Ore.: Multnomah Press, 1983), 238-39.
5. I am indebted to James Bryan Smith for the phrase "flash prayers." See his excellent book *A Spiritual Formation Workbook: Small Group Resources for Nurturing Christian Growth* (San Francisco: HarperSan Francisco, 1993), 66.

Week Ten

1. Many of the insights, especially the background material, on the parable of the Good Samaritan that follow come from three sources: Kenneth E. Bailey, *Through Peasant Eyes*, part of a combined edition of two of his works entitled *Poet and Peasant* and *Through Peasant Eyes* (Grand Rapids, Mich.: Eerdmans, 1976); Walter L. Liefeld, "Luke," in *The Expositor's Bible Commentary*, ed. Frank E. Gaebelein (Grand Rapids, Mich.: Zondervan, 1984), vol.

8; and I. Howard Marshall, *Commentary on Luke*, New International Greek Testament Commentary series (Grand Rapids, Mich.: Eerdmans, 1978). I am particularly indebted to Bailey's work. His book is a superb scholarly explanation of the parables in the Gospel of Luke. It is especially informative when it comes to providing cultural background material that brings the parables alive. While this work is a bit heavy going for beginning Bible students, I highly recommend it for those with more experience in the discipline of Scripture study.

2. Liefeld, 943.
3. Bailey, 46.
4. Mishna *Shebiith* 8:10, as quoted in Bailey, 48.
5. W. O. E. Oesterley, *The Gospel Parables in the Light of Their Jewish Background*, as quoted in Bailey, 48.
6. Bailey, 52-53.
7. William Law, *A Serious Call to a Devout and Holy Life*, John Wesley, ed. quoted in *The Heart of True Spirituality, John Wesley's Own Choice: Volume 1* (Grand Rapids, Mich.: Francis Asbury Press, 1985), 92.
8. Francis of Assisi, *A Day in Your Presence*, readings arranged by David Hazard (Minneapolis: Bethany House, 1992), 53.

SIX: *Confession*

Week Eleven

1. Peter Kreeft, *Making Sense Out of Suffering* (Ann Arbor, Mich.: Servant, 1986), 116.
2. C. S. Lewis, *Mere Christianity* (New York: Macmillan, 1952), 174-75.

Week Twelve

1. See Bailey, 158-206; Liefeld, 983-85; Marshall, 604-13.
2. Charles R. Swindoll, *Improving Your Serve: The Art of Unselfish Living* (Waco, Tex.: Word, 1981), 60-62.
3. Allen C. Guelzo, "Fear of Forgiving," *Christianity Today* (Feb. 8, 1993), 42-43.
4. Lewis B. Smedes, *Forgive and Forget: Healing the Hurts We Don't Deserve* (San Francisco: Harper & Row, 1984), 29.
5. Smedes, 132-33.
6. Lewis, *Mere Christianity*, 118.

ABOUT THE AUTHOR

William D. Watkins is the president of his literary company William Pens; the vice president of the think-tank Liberty, Life and Family Institute; and the director of publications of the public-interest law firm and educational organization called the American Center for Law and Justice. Bill has been involved in the publishing industry for nearly two decades. working for such organizations as Thomas Nelson, Moody Press, Insight for Living, and Probe Ministries.

Among the many books he has written are *The New Absolutes, In Defense of Life,* and *Worlds Apart: A Handbook on World Views.*

He has written many popular and scholarly articles, booklets, and study guides as well. His many articles have appeared in such publications as *Christianity Today, Themelios, Trinity Journal, Law & Justice, Liberty, Life and Family Journal, Dallas/Fort Worth Heritage, Insights, Cornerstone, The Lookout, Christian Research Journal, Moody Magazine,* and *Kindred Spirit.* With best-selling author Charles Swindoll, Bill coauthored more than a dozen study guides. Enjoying devotional writing, he also helped launch the Moody monthly devotional publication *Today in the Word* and the devotional magazine by Search Ministries called *Connexions.* He contributed numerous devotionals to both publications.

Bill is also an often-requested speaker and teacher, covering a wide range of topics from spirituality to parenting, social issues to writing, world views to moral decision-making, dealing with suffering to enjoying life."The Christian world view touches every facet of our lives,"

Bill says. "The more we understand and consistently apply Christianity's truths, the better we will be able to handle life's twists and turns."

For more information about Bill's literary business, Williams Pens or to contact him about teaching or speaking, write:

> William D. Watkins, Rev.
> William Pens
> 342 Alden Cove Drive
> Smyrna, Tennessee 37167